Dr Louise J. Lawrence is currentl
Studies and SWMTC Research Fell
She is author of *An Ethnography of*
Siebeck, 2003), *Reading with Anthropology: Exhibiting Aspects of New Testament Religion* (Paternoster, 2005) and co-editor with Mario Aguilar of *Anthropology and Biblical Studies: Avenues of Approach* (Deo, 2004).

IN LOVING MEMORY OF

THE REVD CHARLES ROBERT LEWIS

(1966–2008)

THE WORD IN PLACE

Reading the New Testament in Contemporary Contexts

LOUISE J. LAWRENCE

First published in Great Britain in 2009

Society for Promoting Christian Knowledge
36 Causton Street
London SW1P 4ST

British Library Cataloguing-in-Publication Data
A catalogue record for this book is available from the British Library

ISBN 978–0–281–06112–9

1 3 5 7 9 10 8 6 4 2

Typeset by Graphicraft Limited, Hong Kong
Printed in Great Britain by Ashford Colour Press

Produced on paper from sustainable forests

Contents

Contents

Illustrations

Foreword

Many of the themes in this book I first heard Louise Lawrence begin to explore in a series of Diocesan Conferences during Lent 2008. Her central theme was a response to the somewhat enigmatic question: 'Are you hefted?' 'Hefted' is a term used to describe sheep that, over many generations, have become so familiar with the land on which they graze, for whom it is so much their home that they do not require fences or sheepdogs to keep them secure. Their knowledge of the terrain is quite enough. However, when the features of the land change dramatically, or when they are moved from familiar territory altogether, they become disorientated and confused; they lose their memory and – quite literally – do not know where to turn next. In that image I found a striking and profound insight into the experience of many Christians and churches in the context of today's culture and society.

Now in this engaging book there is much to stimulate and encourage a faithful Christian exploration and response. Through the insights drawn from different groups of people as they engaged with the same group of gospel readings in different social settings, both text and context receive fresh illumination. In these pages you will find the material for rich reflection on the practice and spirituality of ministry and discipleship, and of the relationship between lay and ordained within the whole economy of the people of God. In offering fresh ways of reading, understanding, exploring and responding to the different situations in which faith has to be lived today, Louise also offers a much needed theological underpinning and investigation of emerging expressions of church life alongside that which is more familiar and better known.

The Rt Revd Michael Langrish
Bishop of Exeter

Acknowledgements

This book is the culmination of a three-year research fellowship sponsored by the South West Ministry Training Course (SWMTC). Thanks to the vision and support of SWMTC I have had the opportunity to work with remarkable people in a variety of contexts across the South West of England. All volunteers have openly shared their stories and experiences with me in response to biblical narratives. I am so grateful to each of them, for without their willing participation this project could never have hoped to move beyond the drawing-board stage. I am indebted to the Revd Julyan Drew, the Revd David Nixon, the Revd Peter Henderson and Prebendary Gill Behenna (Member of the Register of Sign Language Interpreters [MRSLI]) for instigating my work in respective contexts, and in the latter's case for acting as one of the interpreters, along with Rosemary Macro (MRSLI), for sessions with the Deaf group.

The management team of the project deserve special thanks: the Revd David Moss (Principal of SWMTC), Dr Christopher Southgate and Professor David Horrell. I could not have hoped for three wiser, caring or more discerning dialogue partners; it has been both a pleasure and privilege to work so closely with them. Thanks also to other SWMTC staff – the Revd Sue Sheppard, the Revd Canon Dr Stephen Dawes, the Revd Dr John Searle, the Revd Andi Hofbauer and Mrs Patricia Robottom – for their unfailing encouragement and interest in how 'the project' was going. The Department of Theology at the University of Exeter has been 'my place' for the duration of this research. I feel so fortunate to have been able to return to Exeter and work with such super colleagues. Thanks to them not only for granting me research leave to write this book, but also for the daily theology 'coffee' trips where lots of thinking as well as chatting took place!

The Rt Revd Michael Langrish, Bishop of Exeter, has been a great advocate of the project. I am immensely grateful to him for all his guidance and truly honoured that he has written the Foreword for this book. The Rt Revd Bill Ind, the Revd Canon Andrew Godsall and the Revd Peter Chave should also be thanked for the various opportunities they have given to me to introduce some of my findings in public. One of the great joys of the last three years has been sharing my research with churches in general and SWMTC ordinands in particular. The Revd Hilary Dawson should be particularly singled out here. Her MA dissertation on contextual readings among ordinands particularly helped me think through issues for Chapter 8 of this book.

Rebecca Mulhearn, commissioning editor at SPCK, has been a welcome and constant support throughout the whole production process. Some parts of this book have already been published in article form in *Discourse* (Lawrence 2006) and the *Expository Times* (Lawrence 2007a; 2008; 2009). Thanks go to the respective editors and publishers (Higher Education Academy and Sage) for permission to reuse material here. I presented ideas from Chapter 6 of this book in the Contextual Bible Study Seminar at the Society of Biblical Literature annual meeting in San Diego in November 2007, and material in Chapter 7 was first delivered as a paper at the Bible and Social Justice Conference in Sheffield in June 2008. I am appreciative to the hosts of both events for inviting me to participate in them.

On a personal level thanks, as always, to my parents: the 'cardiac hitch' as I began this research seems only to have strengthened us all. They remain, as ever, my life's fortress and stronghold. Thanks also to Dan Morgan who has wholeheartedly bought into the idea of 'heftedness' and without whom any place, for me, would lack love and laughter.

Finally, this book is dedicated to the memory of a former SWMTC student, the Revd Charles Robert Lewis, who was dear to, and respected by, all on the course. Charlie was not only a gifted dramatist, director and educator, but also a person of immense and inspirational faith. He freely and devotedly ministered to others throughout his life, including most powerfully and poignantly his last few weeks at Rowcroft Hospice. I am so sorry Charlie is not here to see the publication of this book, but I think he would have approved of the spirit of the research on which it was built. Charlie understood the importance of the 'word in place' more than most when he reinstituted a number of forgotten local traditions (including Plough Sunday and Queene's Day) in his pastoral work at Berry

Acknowledgements

Pomeroy. His immeasurable legacy will live on in that community for many years to come.

Louise Lawrence
University of Exeter

Introduction

Stories are the currency of ordinary history ... they help us to share
knowledge of what makes a place.

Sue Clifford and Angela King

Stories and memories, both remarkable and mundane, connect
people and places in assorted and surprising ways. Figure 1.1, for
example, displays an iconic image of Hallsands, a village in the South
Hams, which, following dredging of 650,000 tons of shingle to ex-
pand Devonport Dockyard, was swept into the sea one stormy night
in January 1917. Guidebooks of the area call the disaster 'a testament to man's folly' and a recent book entitled *Hallsands: A Village
Betrayed* (Melia 2002) witnesses to the catastrophic loss to the villagers, their ultimately unsuccessful campaign against the dredging,
and the political cover-up that ensued following the tragedy. Today
only the skeleton profiles of a few houses on the cliff can be seen.
They stand as eerie reminders of humanity's intense and fragile
relationship with the places they inhabit and are haunting 'ghosts'
of humanity's [ab]use of creation. This story, like many others, from
different places the world over, continues to engage and inspire.
William Stanton based his award-winning play *Foul Tide* on the disaster, for in his words, 'I wanted to examine the issues ... of greed
and helplessness and what is sometimes sacrificed to the perceived
greater good, in this case national security' (2005:10). Hallsands is,
like many other places, effectively 'dead' as a consequence of the
domination of one particular mythology (national security) and the
muting of the villagers' alternative voices (based on intimate knowledge of the coastline) on the ground.

To read particular biblical narratives 'alongside' such contexts and
disputes is to unlock a whole new potential meaning for biblical
stories. Similar to the disciples who were fearful for their lives on a
storm-ravaged Lake Galilee, monstrously chaotic seas and fragile
cliff faces could provide powerful commentaries not just on places
that have experienced annihilating catastrophe on the level of
Hallsands, but also on a variety of other social situations. It is not

Figure 1.1 The lost village of Hallsands

only the spectacular or tragic but also the ordinary and 'common-
place' that make up the fabric of our contexts and indelibly mark
our outlooks and interpretations. As such, this book takes as its
starting point the anthropological insight that the human being is
a 'story-telling animal' (Novak 1975). Through sharing narratives,
humans make sense of the world and their environments. But
stories are not told in a vacuum but always 'in context'; in this

respect they can corroborate and identify with, or challenge and subvert, alternative stories or mythologies: 'large-scale narratives that engage our imaginations and shape the way we experience the world' (Ramachandra 2008:12). Christians are of course 'a storied people', called to live out, and make visible, 'good news' in their lives. Christian mission itself demands narration of 'a unique vision of humanness in the teeth of all the other definitions of humanness that abound in the mass media, the academy and the business world' (Ramachandra 2008:104). The Christian story has accordingly recently offered alternative perspectives to dominant cultural narratives surrounding the war on terror, global capitalism and multiculturalism. Such interactions demand that the context and situations in which stories are told, and promoted, be given due attention.

It is one dominant 'mythology' that particularly interests me here, for it has led to widespread 'dislocation': namely the Western industrialized world's breeding of increasingly transitory ways of living and the resultant ideological 'displacement' of many. Anthropologists have, in response to these trends, constructed 'place' as involving shared corporate narratives and embodied interactions and negatively contrasted these with 'non-places', vacuums devoid of such interdependent pursuits. In a bid to save the Church from ever taking on the characteristics of non-places so prevalent within our society, recent theology has also taken 'place' and 'place-making' as a priority for reflection, for Christians are called to embody the Kingdom of God, *here* on earth. Moreover, Christianity is at base a profoundly material religion: the incarnation conceives of the divine 'moving into the neighbourhood' (as a recent popular translation of John 1.14 puts it, *The Message* (Peterson 2002)) and in so doing poses the radical invitation to communities to discover the word in their own place. Often reflections on 'place' help build relationships and provide contexts for dialogue about important issues within a community, particularly in instances where there is conflict. It also allows space for people both to voice 'stories of discontent' and/or corporately imagine new stories for the kind of future their place is to have. As such, this book documents various 'Contextual Bible Studies' on passages from the Gospel of Luke that I have conducted among a variety of contemporary communities in places linked by location (inner-city areas, rural villages), experience (the Deaf community) and vocation (the fishing industry and clergy). Encounters with these biblical narratives through the Contextual Bible Study process encouraged communities to transform and challenge other stories which promoted 'non-place' or 'displacement' within their experience. Building on the bedrock of this fieldwork this book also offers resources for other contemporary communities to think about their relationships to particular 'places' and interpret selected biblical texts from these perspectives. The book is accordingly subdivided into three main parts: (Part I) 'People, places and stories'; (Part II) 'Reading the New Testament in contemporary contexts'; (Part III) 'The word in place: prospects and possibilities'.

Part I: People, places and stories

Chapter 1, 'Recovering a sense of place', documents the Western world's disintegration of 'a sense of place' and draws on recent theological reflection that offers avenues to 'construct place'. Given the centrality of 'story' among the various theological contributions, I suggest that contextual reflection on scripture may be one important way to develop and inculcate the virtue of 'place-making' wherever you happen to be. Chapter 2, 'The folk arts of biblical interpretation: introducing contextual readings', elucidates a method by which this sort of reflection can be done: Contextual Bible Study. Drawing inspiration from liberation theology's move to read the Bible in grass-roots base communities, Contextual Bible Study was developed for use in small community groups in post-apartheid South Africa and has since been fruitfully employed throughout the world. The method prioritizes 'community/folk consciousness' responses to biblical texts that draw on the experiences, location and culture of the participants. Only after these have been probed are 'critical consciousness' responses (literary, historical and sociological) addressed. Variously in such projects, the possibilities of 'folk' theologies have been showcased. Christ has been revealed as the Malawian faith-healer (Musopole 1993) and a balm for the 'dis-ease' of AIDS spreading throughout the African continent (West 2003); the Psalms have been seen as performative acts akin to healing words in Nigeria (Adamo 2004); the Syro-Phoenician woman's humility has given voice to the Dalit woman's subjection to verbal abuse by a landlord (Nelavala 2006); Jerusalem's demise recorded in Lamentations has spoken to the fallen and their kin in the Tiananmen Square massacre

(Lee 2004); Mary and Elizabeth's loss of their sons has struck a chord with the grief of inmates at Stirling Women's Prison in Scotland who have had their children taken away and placed into social care (Peden 2005). Collectively such interpretations provide powerful responses to the invitation to discern the 'word' in particular places and in contrast to other dominating contemporary myths. Chapter 3, 'Reading in place: approaches and methods', will provide practical tips and resources for initiating contextual readings within a variety of communities. Four main themes related to place – 'home', 'those out of place', 'sustainability' and 'displacement' – will be introduced as frameworks for the study. Ethnography will also be posited as a method by which 'readings' of communities can occur alongside 'readings' of texts, and what I have termed a 'hermeneutics of presence' (a pattern of interpretation based on 'being with' others) can be developed.

Part II: Reading the New Testament in contemporary contexts

Part II will showcase some of the dynamics of selected contextual biblical readings that I have been privileged to gather in my research: from a city regeneration area, a rural village, a fishing village, a group of Deaf people, and groups of clergy. These interpretations demonstrate not only the variety of potential meanings that a biblical text can birth, but also practically demonstrate the process of 'place-making' through the collective responses to the biblical texts within the groups. Many interpretations referred not only to personal experiences but also local histories, experiences and culture, and involved a variety of media and activities (including mapping, art and performance), intentionally 're-membering' the cultural heritages of the participants that have in the past been expressed in painting, performance, folk tale and festival, as well as 'words' alone. Although the majority of groups in which I worked were Christian, some included agnostics and non-church attendees. This move was intentional, as place (understood variously as geographical, experiential or vocational), rather than religion, was what primarily united participants in this study. Each group, as will be seen, also referred to dominant constructions or mythologies operative within their culture (social exclusion, rural idyll etc.). Many participants echoed these uncritically but others took up the challenge within the group-work to tease out alternative 'gospel-inspired' perspectives.

It should also be noted that it is not only within community settings where the contributions of this contextual approach have been recognized; the guild of biblical studies is also increasingly aware of the importance of readings that draw the original context of the text and the contemporary context of the reader into dialogue. Lisa Cahill testifies to this when she states, 'biblical scholars have become more explicitly aware of the social repercussions of [their interpretations] and also more interested in drawing social and moral analogies between the biblical world and our own' (Cahill 1990:384). As such, an important dimension of the contextual reflections presented will be to initiate a dynamic dialogue between the biblical texts and the respective contemporary contexts in which these are read.

Part III: The word in place: prospects and possibilities

This section will draw some comparative conclusions regarding the fieldwork outlined above. It will be proposed that allegory, parable and midrashic techniques link many contextual responses and these modes of reading may be key tools in the construction of what could be termed a 'hermeneutics of place'. Diverse reactions to the various Christologies presented within the different biblical narratives will also be broached and finally an agenda for 'Christian place-making' will be presented. Rowan Williams, writing at the turn of the millennium, urged Christians to concern themselves 'as best as they can in those enterprises in their culture that seek to create or recover a sense of shared discourse and common purpose in human society' (Williams 2000:37). Stimulated by discussions initiated here, reflection by contemporary communities on local culture and context in reference to biblical texts seems one particularly promising response to this plea.

Part I

PEOPLE, PLACES AND STORIES

1

Recovering a sense of place

If we were able to rediscover the significance of place, vital aspects of our humanity would be renewed.

John Inge

Human bodies occupy 'places'. The very name 'human', deriving as it does from the Latin *humus*, meaning 'earth', makes it clear that we are intimately connected to our terrain. I am typing this manuscript upstairs in my parents' house; I cannot be simultaneously at a seminar in the university or running along the beach, for I am here, in this setting, at this moment. Whether breathtaking and beautiful or austere and unsightly, these places, the settings of our embodied experiences, constitute 'the fabric of everyday lives, structuring our memories, determining our attitudes' (Gorringe 2002:1). Anthropologists, cultural geographers and psychologists have variously recorded some link between 'who we are' and 'where we are'. The human being in many respects could quite properly be called a 'topophiliac', 'a place lover' (a term coined by Tuan 1974:4).

Theorists tell us however that 'place' is not a concept that should be understood solely in spatial terms – this place 'here' or 'over there' – but also as a verb. We talk about ambition as 'going places', define our psychological state as being in a 'good or bad place', and censor others by 'putting them in their place'. Place is therefore a 'construction' performed, reproduced and modified in practice, dialogue, shared experiences and stories (both fictional and biographical). The link with stories makes explicit the fact that places are not neutral – 'they are occupied by some people's stories but not by others' (Sheldrake 2001:20) – as such places can be sites of contradiction, paradox and contest as much as concord. To use Arjun Appardurai's evocative imagery, people are not 'incarcerated' in places, they are rather involved in 'constructing them' as embodied, gendered, inscribed and contested (1988).

The relationship between story and the construction of place is well attested in ethnographies across the world. Indeed the word 'narrative' is derived from an Indo-European root, *gna*, which means both 'to tell' and 'to know' (Hinchman and Hinchman 2001:xiii). This is in part due to the recognition of the importance of stories in forging collectives or communities. Anthropologists time and again reveal that the 'placed' peoples of the world not only told, but ritually re-enacted, parts of their communal story, effectively becoming in themselves 'place-like'. For example, aboriginal house plans facilitated the production and consumption of food by large groups and thus promoted primitive communism (Low and Lawrence 1990: 456). In a related vein, Guinea coast cosmology posits a relationship between settlement areas and forests and saw these as mirroring the bond between the visible world of mortals and the invisible world of the spirits (Jedrej 1996:548). The Dogon conceived of village structures in anthropomorphic terms, 'the plan of a house representing a man lying on his side procreating' (Low and Lawrence-Zuniga 2003:4). In the philosopher Stephen Crite's words,

> such stories and the symbolic worlds they project are *not like monuments that men behold, but like dwelling places. People live in them . . .* They are moving forms, at once musical and narrative, which inform people's sense of the story of which their own lives are a part.
>
> (my italics, Crites 2001[1971]:31)

Many anthropologists accordingly posit a 'sense of place' as a crucial vehicle for conceiving of one's own community as a discrete body, for places are nexuses of value, experience and desires of a people (see Tuan 1977).

Despite the relevant import of place, however, many have recognized that increasingly people in the West are living 'out of place' in one sense or another. While our forebears took rootedness as a certainty (born, working and worshipping in one place, eating locally produced crops, enjoying a network of support from fellow residents and at the last being buried with the ancestors in the local graveyard) we now live in a mobile, technological, individualistic and increasingly rootless world. In the words of one commentator, 'we have since the Second World War de-emphasised place for the sake of values such as mobility, centralisation and economic rationalisation'

(Sheldrake 2001:8; see also Markusen 2004). While the evolution of the industrialized 'global village' has undoubtedly reaped economic 'booty' and re-imagined relationships through electronic forums, it is also true that such developments have not come without a price on the local level, often 'disengaging' people, if not physically certainly psychologically, from their immediate communities and land (see Percy 2006:3–15). The very notion of 'commuter villages' and 'dormitory towns' speaks of increasingly transitory ways of living. Such movements pull against the possibilities of human interactions, and when communities don't communicate not only is a rich vein of experience left unmined, they also literally forget who they collectively are. The world is increasingly suffering from this corporate amnesia and does so at its peril. James Speth similarly lists factors in the Western world that have created a displacement of people and the creation of 'placelessness'. These include population growth, technology, poverty, cultural values and globalization (Speth 2004 in Bouma-Prediger and Walsh 2008:171). The 'commodity' nature of 'dwelling places' in Western society is seen in the ridiculousness of brand new building developments whose advertising boards can jarringly state 'Welcome home' (McHugh 2003:169).

The French anthropologist Marc Augé has as a result of these trends identified what he terms 'non-place' (*non-lieux*) in Western culture, vacuums bereft of story or community: chain supermarkets, cloned shopping malls and airports. In Augé's opinion the person occupying a non-place 'retrieves his identity only at customs, at the tollbooth, at the checkout counter. Meanwhile he obeys the same codes as others, receives the same messages, and responds to the same entreaties; the space of non-place creates neither singular identity nor relations, only solitude and similitude' (Augé 1995:103). In non-place one becomes desensitized to the importance of bonds of relationships, histories and experiences with others in the same location. In our various transit and non-place states, stories are not communicated and social relationships are at best suspended, at worst made extinct. We are in essence 'exiles' for 'no place is like home' and all places are disposable. In the provocative title of James Kunstler's work, we inhabit *The Geography of Nowhere* (1993). We mix and confuse localities and export 'Disney' and 'McDonald's' imagination worldwide (Relph 1976). It could be said that in non-place, Disney constitutes a 'middle-class pilgrimage site' whose cross-referencing and utopian aspects 'appeal to people's need in later capitalist society' (Low 1996:396).

The internet and cyberspace deserve attention at this point for we are undoubtedly also 'in an era of technospheric space' (Mannur 2003:283). Dispersed and distant individuals meet and 'chat' about interests, from Ducati racing bikes to bonsai trees, and even date in virtual realms. These 'cyberscapes' necessarily preclude interaction in person. It is perhaps an irony then that the most popular social networking sites in virtual reality are called 'MySpace' and 'Facebook' but never involve any embodied, face-to-face interaction at all; you can be 'virtually' anyone. Samuel Wilson and Leighton Peterson (2002), in their anthropological study of online communication, reveal that the internet has allowed new types of social bonds to emerge. They support the identification of online worlds as constituting 'communities' linked by interest, not geography, on the basis that not all communities depend on face-to-face interaction (nationalism for instance transcends such exchanges), so 'online communities' likewise can 'merge and repollinate one another in virtual realms' (Mannur 2003:283). Wilson and Peterson also reveal how the internet has been used in some instances to challenge political hierarchies (by providing an alternative 'media' communication) and in the process re-energize 'citizen based democracy' (2002:451). On the other side of the coin, however, they are also swift to warn against anomic violence, the promotion of damaging ideologies within online forums and the dangers of the blurring of boundaries between the virtual realm and embodied reality. In 2008, media coverage of a married couple citing grounds for divorce as a cyber-affair in the online game Second Life illustrates these 'displacing' threats.

Forging the 'non-place' into 'place' is a priority like never before. This involves creating community and sharing collective wisdom about our relationships and immediate locality: for stories of place must start with the personal, the particular and the vernacular, 'rather than the anonymous or disengaged' (Sheldrake 2001:22). This begs the question: what means are there available to us to listen to particular stories from all sections of society and in effect 'cultivate place'?

Theology and the recovery of a sense of place

Theology has of course got an important contribution to offer to the rehabilitation of a sense of place. Religion traditionally not only demarcated particular sites and buildings as sacred and holy, but also recognized that certain environments and locations are particularly adept at promoting spiritual reflection. The Desert Fathers found mystical solace in wilderness landscapes; others received revelation and enlightenment on mountains. Jerusalem and Rome are celebrated as foundational places for Christian history; cathedrals and churches, monasteries and shrines, sites of visions and healings are marked as places of piety, religious devotion and power. However, a common criticism is that theology still is more preoccupied with time (particularly notions of end time) rather than place. John Inge's recent book, *A Christian Theology of Place* (2003), sets out to redress this imbalance. Inge makes an important distinction between 'spaces', which he sees as undifferentiated husks that are empty of meaning, and 'places', which are known and endowed with meaning and value. He follows Christianity's history as 'the most material of the world religions', positing matter as an 'instrument of the spirit' (2003:64) and the world as 'a theatre of God's actions' (2003:85). From Celtic spirituality to pilgrimages, from ritual to tradition, Christian reflection has helped to reinforce the permanency of particular sacred places (2003:84). Church buildings in England are consequently seen as places of 'substantial renewal', reminding people of the particular story of the encounters with the divine that have taken place there (2003:122). In Inge's opinion, the basis for this is sacramental:

> The power of a particular place, associated with its past, will not be mediated by 'conscious reflection' but by a much more integrated attention of the sort mediated by sacrament and symbol. There is, after all our attempt to clarify, a mystery associated with the power of places that is better articulated by poetry than rational argument . . . We can be clear that when a place is sacralized, the dimensions of history become added to personal identity and individual experience, giving it a particular cultural cognizance . . . holiness is built into the *story of a place* so that the Christian community can be built up in faith by association with it.
> (my italics, 2003:86)

In a related vein, Philip Sheldrake, in his *Spaces for the Sacred: Place, Memory and Identity* (2001), identified the importance of story in reflecting on place both theologically and spiritually. One important aspect of Sheldrake's argument for present purposes is to connect different places to history in general and narrative in particular. On one level Sheldrake sees that physical places are vital sources of metaphors for our social constructions of reality; but he also notes that 'the meaning of places unfold in stories, myths [and] rituals' and 'the social significance of places finds expression in music, art and architecture' (2001:6). Thus in his opinion every place is overflowing with meaning and cannot be fully encapsulated in one story or single evaluation. Rather, in the interpretation of place, topography, story and memories are formed and transformed in each particular moment. Sheldrake also realizes that in a contemporary world of exiles and displaced peoples, to engender an effective narrative of place will involve creating 'room for the unheard or marginalized' (2001:22). He accordingly identifies the Eucharist as a 'sacrament of equals' of the placed body of Christ, a body that can physically as well as spiritually transform 'empty' spaces that foster atomism rather than togetherness.

Some recent works have sought explicitly to engage with places other than those traditionally seen as 'sacred' to develop place-making sensitivities. David Brown's book, *God and Enchantment of Place* (2004), berates the fact that theology has largely withdrawn from areas of 'human experience that were once religion's concern' (Brown 2004:5): sports, gardens, art and architecture etc. He in effect widens the parameters of possible places for encounter with the divine:

> To ask what practical purpose a particular building style serves or to reduce gardening or sport to questions of exercise or relaxation is already to distort their potential. The capacity for opening us to a world of divine enchantment lies precisely in resisting such pressures.
>
> (Brown 2004:408)

He also exposes the exclusive focus on God's relationship to human-kind within recent theology to the neglect of place and petitions for a renewed interest in the latter for 'engendering a sense of divine presence' (2004:24). For Brown, 'cities are more than just the sum of the individuals who happen to live there. Buildings and the layout of cities can also help initiate experience of God, and this is an insight which the contemporary church has largely lost' (2004:177). Brown posits a sacramental approach to place, but petitions that the spiritual dimension should not be confused with the aesthetic. God's enchantment can be seen in the ordinary and plain just as much as the extraordinary and lovely.

Timothy Gorringe's celebrated work, *A Theology of the Built Environment* (2002), also argues for the potential revelatory character of all places. Buildings from garden sheds to housing estates speak volumes about morality, social justice and divine presence. Gorringe literally sees 'structural sin' in those built environments that do not foster human flourishing, equality or sensory delight. Citing Nicholas Wolterstorff he submits, 'we have adopted a pietistic-materialistic understanding ... viewing human needs as the need for a saved soul plus the need for food, clothes and shelter. True shalom is vastly richer than that' (Gorringe 2002:10). Akin to Brown, Gorringe also sees theology's retreat from issues such as planning and development as a limiting censorship of contexts in which God is met. In his words,

> The built environment reflects not just ideologies but, in Wink's terms, spiritualities. Profound, creative, grace-filled spiritualities produce grace-filled environments; banal, impoverished, alienated spiritualities produce alienating environments. If that is the case, and I believe it is undeniable, then theology is anything but incidental to the debate about the built environment that is such a vital dimension of the human future. (Gorringe 2002:24)

Gorringe petitions theologians to look beyond cathedrals and deserts for divine encounters and realize that these are but 'potent reminders of the potential for epiphany of *all* other spaces' (my italics, Gorringe 2002:40). Gorringe (2007) has also picked up on social-scientific literature regarding the erosion of place into non-place in Western contexts. Reflecting critically on the built environment of Blackbird Leys, a dismal and decaying council estate in Oxford, he helpfully sets out points for 'place-making' or remedying the threat of 'non-place' in the future. First, citing Kunstler, Gorringe submits that 'the culture of good place making, like the culture of farming or agriculture, is a body of knowledge and acquired skills. It is not bred in the bone and if it is not transmitted from one generation to the next, it is lost' (Kunstler cited in Gorringe 2007). Second, he submits that place-making always involves the empowerment of the people in the locality. They must feel their voice is heard and listened to, for disempowerment perpetuates silence and social atomism. Third, Gorringe submits that a satisfying place cannot be made without justice. This means that each person, no matter how long they have lived in an area, or what social level they are from, must be viewed and treated as stakeholders in the sense of place and community. Fourth, Gorringe argues that place-making involves either the recapturing or the creation of the charm of places and from that the will to sustain them through specific practices. Attractive design and facilities for community interaction are essential. Fifth, he submits in Christian terms that the Church should be a place-maker par excellence, for it must always strive for the realization of the Kingdom on earth. Although 'utopia' literally translates as 'non-place', the vision of the New Jerusalem should never be complacently dismissed, but always set forth as a goal to be at least in part realized on earth. All five place-making activities in many ways involve giving each person a voice within their place and reflecting on the ethos by which community and environment is developed and sustained. A trinitarian framework that conceives of persons in relationship underwrites this place-making agenda.

Steven Bouma-Prediger and Brian Walsh's recent volume, *Beyond Homelessness: Christian Faith in a Culture of Displacement* (2008), develops some of the themes of Gorringe's project and suggests ways in which a Christian culture of 'homecoming' could be developed. Drawing once more on the importance of 'living into story' to create what they term 'homecoming' virtues, they focus on four particular qualities. The first virtue is peace, which, following Jesus' example, is sacrificial. This seeks non-violent means to challenge the destructive powers and myths of the day and 'expose the emptiness of consumerism and materialism, not with an air of condemnation but in the pursuit of conciliation' (2008:14). Second, and echoing Gorringe's programme, is justice. True shalom has justice and equity at heart, but also a realization that the manifestation of justice will be different according to particular situations: 'the virtue of justice is the settled supposition to treat others fairly, rooted in wisdom and respect' (2008:216). Third is the virtue of compassion, which at base demands a 'being with' rather than 'working on behalf of' people who suffer. True compassion works in the mess of real life; it is the opposite of apathy that is literally 'to lack feeling' (2008:220). Fourth, and in some respects most important, is wisdom. Bouma-Prediger and Walsh posit this virtue not as intelligence, 'know how' or educational prowess, but rather 'the ability to discern paths of shalom in the midst of competing visions and conflicting interests' (2008:222). It is the ability to differentiate the Christian call of 'homecoming' above alternative cultural stories promoting 'homelessness'.

All the authors above centre in some way on the importance of Christians as a storied people, through whom these four virtues are cultivated. It is no coincidence then that the decline of narrative identity was recognized by some theorists as a symptom of the decline in place attachment. Lewis and Sandra Hinchman reveal that 'what we often perceive as a loss of meaning amounts, then, to the eclipse of narrative knowledge as such, and its replacement by other forms of cognition, especially technological ones' (Hinchman and Hinchman 2001:xiii). Christians must, in this light, re-inhabit the story of scripture and develop the wisdom to discern the word in their place.

Recovering a sense of place in Contextual Bible Study

The equation between place and narrative, memory and story can be forged in Contextual Bible Study that works in groups within local contexts and prioritizes community consciousness responses to biblical texts. Implicit within this model is the belief that talking about the authority of scripture is to talk primarily about acceptance of scripture as a story, which people can, to differing degrees, inhabit and which can in turn transform their vision of their own context. Contextual Bible Study promotes communal 'storied identity' and in the words of Richard Bauckham 'does not simply require assent':

> Like all stories it [the Bible] draws us into its world, engages us imaginatively, and allows us at our own pace to grow accustomed to it . . . But it leaves the story open to the inclusion of all other stories; including those we play some part in writing.   (Bauckham 2002:65)

Promises of such a method are many. It articulates a positive response to the five areas identified by Gorringe for place-making. For scripture is a story that specific communities can choose to inhabit to collectively formulate wisdom. Like place, scripture overflows with potential meanings 'and invites all other stories to find the ending that will give them meaning in the coming Kingdom of God' (Bauckham 2002:76). Bouma-Prediger and Walsh likewise see promoted within scripture the virtues central to Christian homecoming: peace, justice, compassion and wisdom.

It is important to state at the outset that I am not seeking to promote a romanticized vision of belonging to place. Quite the contrary, I acknowledge that often areas that have a very strong place identity are not the most functional community environments, for place attachment can too often lapse into a resistance to change, a suspicion of the other or in extreme cases violent territorialism. I am also not denying the fact that biblical narratives have frequently been employed in 'oppressive' spatial policies. Indeed the origins of Contextual Bible Study, as will be seen in the following chapter, attests to the way in which the Bible had been employed for good and ill in apartheid contexts. I am grateful to Jo Carruthers who in a response to a paper I gave in Bristol brought to my attention that A. D. Smith had pointed to Israel's election as a key element in the configuration of particular national (and nationalist) identities. 'Israel' has been evoked by the Orange Order in Northern Ireland and the Afrikaners in South Africa to support possessive land claims (Carruthers 2007). The challenge, however, in contextual readings is to tease out specific stories which contribute to constructive dialogues and produce alternative perspectives on extreme positions. Contextual Bible Study also takes seriously the provisional and active sense of place: namely how some stories can disrupt certain places, and how stories themselves are in turn disrupted by a sense of place. The return to the local and particular also allows one to see how, in different contexts, people are enabled to 'live into' biblical texts and discover alternative visions from those (damaging ones) promoted in their contexts, hopefully to foster the Kingdom on earth.

2

The folk arts of biblical interpretation: introducing contextual readings

> Folk artist – searching for expression . . . through symbols, forms
> and movements that are capable of capturing and transforming the
> imaginations of a particular community.
>
> Leonora Tubbs Tisdale

There is a certain amount of truth in the observation that 'context
is the sea we swim in'. It is not only our physical environment but
also the symbolic arena in which we make sense of the world. *The
Oxford English Dictionary* reveals the origin of the word 'context' from
the Latin *con*, meaning 'with', and *texere*, meaning 'to weave'. Within
biblical studies a major preoccupation within the historical-critical
paradigm has been to capture the intricate 'weave' of the original
first-century contexts in which New Testament texts were produced
(i.e. what a text *meant*). Latterly reader-response paradigms have
increasingly focused on the role of the reader's context in interpretation (i.e. what a text *means*). It is now widely accepted that an interpreter's context inevitably affects meaning – everyone interprets
from somewhere, no one approaches the text without presupposi-
tions. Moreover texts have a variety of meaning 'potentials' according to the diverse contexts in which they are read. Recent advocacy
approaches to the Bible (postcolonial, feminist, queer etc.) have, for
example, proudly worn their specific agendas on their sleeve, variously reforming or resisting biblical interpretations which impact on
their contemporary concerns.

The focus on how a text and its interpretation have marginalized
particular groups of readers has also raised important concerns
regarding the ideological contexts in which texts were not only produced but also subsequently used and read. Biblical interpreters are
now alive to the way in which the Bible has served certain colonial
and class interests, gender prejudices and power hierarchies in social,
ecclesiastical and political institutions. As such, in William Yarchin's

terms, 'the results of biblical interpretation are no longer restricted to understanding the world that created the Bible. The quest now extends more broadly to include the world the Bible has created' (Yarchin 2004:xxix). Moreover the issue of power – 'whose interpretations are viewed as "official", "legitimate" and "superior" and whose are ignored?' – also arises in light of these readings. Brian Blount submits that interpreters occupying a centrist position will not typically engage with the periphery (Blount 1995:23). Yet attention to 'peripheral' contexts of interpretation has of course also exposed the fallacy of objectivity in 'centrist' readings and questioned the belief that any reading (even an historical one) can ever be 'context-less', for 'one's sociohistorical context influences what one sees in language. Every investigative exercise, historical-critical and literary included, has a powerful interpersonal component' (Blount 1995:39). James Cone, in his celebrated work *God of the Oppressed*, gives voice to this in his conclusion that 'what people think about God cannot be divorced from their place and time in a definite history and culture' (1997:37).

However, it is in so-called 'global' readings drawn from the developing world where the rehabilitation of 'peripheral' vernacular voices has been most explicitly pursued in biblical interpretation. These contextual readings, largely motivated as a resistance to colonial impositions of the Bible that neglected, even dismissed, indigenous cultures and stories, have read texts anew in light of local concerns and have exposed imperialist and colonial ideologies. Itumeleng Mosala, for example, chastises the evangelist Luke, and those interpreting his text, for an elitist agenda that makes the poor mere pawns in the moral virtue of the rich (Mosala 1989). Just as Lazarus sits inert, inactive and voiceless at the gate of the rich man, so Africa is objectified and depersonalized in Western analyses. Similarly, Musa Dube chastises the reception of Matthew's Gospel's mission charge as colonial propaganda to make disciples of all nations and racially making dog-like (literally 'canine-izing') the Canaanite woman (Dube 2000). Benny Tat-Siong Liew, who grew up in colonial Hong Kong, critiques the imperial mimicry, or neo-colonialism, inspired by the Gospel of Mark, with language of power and lordship (2006). Such projects testify that whose 'stories' are heard is not an innocent pursuit but rather part of a complex network of power.

Such critiques also laid the foundation for constructive work on the ground level that encouraged local communities to contextualize stories within their own 'place'. Walter Dietrich and Ulrich Luz's edited volume *The Bible in a World Context: An Experiment in Contextual Hermeneutics* (2002) is emblematic of such an approach. The contributions written from the perspective of authors in Costa Rica, Nigeria and Japan respectively all petition for exegesis that is academically informed, pastorally sensitive and engaged with grassroots Christian communities. Daniel Patte's celebrated *The Global Bible Commentary* (2004) likewise initiates specifically 'folk' readings of biblical books through a tripolar method of interaction between (a) the scriptural text, (b) the believers' life context, (c) the believers' religious perceptions of life ('believers' incidentally always being conceived in a communal as opposed to individualistic sense). To demonstrate this more concretely here I will briefly outline four particular cultural contexts (Latin American, African, Indian, Western) to give a brief taste of some of the folk interpretations that have been generated.

The gospel in Latin America

It was liberation theology's move to read the Bible among the poor in Christian base communities in Latin America that first championed a bias for the 'marginal' reader's context and his or her own 'place-based' interpretations. These kind of readings initiated what Stephen Fowl and Gregory Jones would later define as 'a reading of the world alongside a reading of the text' (1991:44). Liberation readings highlighted the unique insights that a reader experiencing social poverty could have in interpreting the Bible. Such readings were used as stimuli for social change and transformation within communities. The method echoed Paulo Freire's educational perspective whereby those silenced by dominant culture were given tools to develop a critical consciousness and thereby work towards liberation and transformation.

Ernesto Cardenal's now famous collection of responses to biblical narratives among peasants in Nicaragua, *The Gospel in Solentiname*, stands as a stunning example of 'contextualizing' scripture in a contemporary reading community. In the collections, presented in dialogues, the *campesinos* interpret Jesus politically, seeing his revolutionary and counter-cultural ethos as a pattern for societal critique in their own situation. Every Sunday Cardenal initiated conversations about the Gospels with the peasants, in which they began to see the vision of the Kingdom as one in which the exploited were liberated from oppression and all goods were held in common. Moreover these interpretations, in Cardenal's opinion, 'taught us that the word of God is not only to be heard, but also put into practice' (Cardenal 1982:272). The community also produced a number of artistic representations of biblical narratives including the massacre of the infants, where the slaughterers were armed with guns instead of swords and decked in the uniform of Somoza Debayle's National Guard. At all times the focus was on practical as opposed to theoretical exegesis: theology, salvation and Christology were not seen as ahistorical, but rather potent stimulants for social change.

The gospel in Africa

If Latin American base communities effectively contextualized biblical narratives in their own contexts and used them as stimulants for emancipation, it was Gerald West, working in the University of Natal, South Africa, who formalized the method. The Contextual Bible Study movement was nurtured in the townships of South Africa during the apartheid era as a force of liberation. The movement, like base-community readings in Latin America, sought to engage folk readers with no specific training in biblical study in contemplative conversation with the text and to value readers' experience as a stimulant for both knowledge and social praxis. In the Institute for the Study of the Bible and Worker Ministry Project 'Doing Contextual Bible Study Resource Manual' (available online – see Bibliography), West reveals that two types of questions lead the so-called Contextual Bible Study process. First are 'community/folk consciousness questions', which draw on the experience and feelings of the participants. Second are 'critical consciousness questions', which include reference to literary, historical and sociological paradigms. The sessions follow the same procedure and notably, akin to the liberation paradigm, have a bias towards the perspective of communities on the borders of society and an explicit emphasis on praxis as the outcome of biblical interpretation. A typical session would run according to the following framework: (a) a reading of

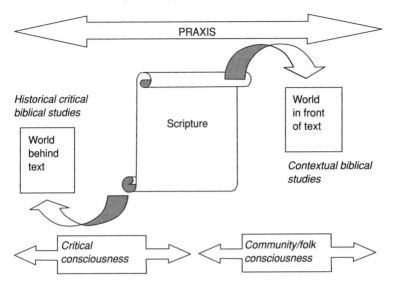

Figure 2.1 Contextual Bible Study methodology

the biblical story and collection of first impressions from the participants; (b) questions on the story with no specialist knowledge
assumed; (c) further analysis of the story and recognition of the story's
potential contribution to wisdom regarding contemporary concerns;
(d) community action (praxis) on the basis of discussion. Figure 2.1
shows how the process can be figuratively envisaged.

Through methods such as these, other African readers found key
resonance between the culture and experiences contained in biblical
narratives and their own. The African in poverty looked to the story
of the Exodus for liberation. For others, Israel's structures based in
kinship and politics found ready resonance with African social and
familial models and a reverence for the relationship between the
land, the divine and the people. John Mbiti, in his book *African
Religion and Philosophy*, even went so far as to claim that 'Christianity can rightly be described as an indigenous, traditional and
African religion' (Mbiti 1975:229). Mario Aguilar, in his work on
1 Maccabees, has also revealed three touchstones with the original
biblical contexts and the diverse African contexts in which he
worked. First, they both held a prevalent belief in the power of spirits and witchcraft. Augustine Musopole (1993) has likewise revealed
Christ as the *sing'anga*, horn of salvation and Malawian faith healer.

Second, Aguilar identifies the collective focus of the communities and the remembrance of ancestors in song and sacrifice within the living family. Citing Francois Kabasele Lumbala, Aguilar contends, 'the ancestors are the first who received the force of life from God. Having passed through death, they are more powerful than living persons, enjoying the capacity to exercise the force of life' (F. Kabasele Lumbala 1998, cited in Aguilar 2002:14). It is no coincidence in this light that Matthias' death speech in 1 Maccabees is prefaced by a list of the ancestors and that he is buried in the ancestral tomb (1 Macc. 2.69). It is also unsurprising that many Africans interpret Christ as the proto-ancestor. Finally, Aguilar identifies a time orientation that is focused primarily on the past and present (as opposed to the future), so much so that in times of trouble and uncertainty origin myths are often used as a source of comfort.

Musa Dube's 'Semoya' (of the spirit) reading strategy similarly initiated contextual readings among women in the African Independent Church. They integrated indigenous religious traditions within their interpretation. By speaking about Moya, the ancestral spirit, within interpretation they started to integrate African religion elements with Christian theology (Dube 2000:189). They also used songs, dramatized narration and rhythm literally to embody a communal interpretation.

The gospel in India

One generative group for folk readings within India has been the Dalits (literally the broken, 'outcastes' and untouchables). Sathianathan Clarke comments specifically on their 'subaltern' reading context. Particularly in light of widespread illiteracy among this sector of the population, the Bible is often viewed as a 'native talisman', that is, an object which is sacred, iconic and powerful, used in healing and meditation – not 'literally' read, but understood through 'touch' and performance, it dramatizes salvation rather than becoming a focus for inward-orientated piety. This performance-orientated hermeneutic (as opposed to a literary, textual one) is often encountered within subaltern or oral contexts. This is further reinforced by the fact that often untouchables are denied physical access to the Hindu Vedas, so Christian missionaries, by allowing free communication of the Bible, effectively made it a tool of liberation. Like the

Latin American and African folk interpreters, Dalit interpretation also tends to contextualize biblical images and stories through experience. M. Gnanavaram, for example, reads the parable of the good Samaritan as liberatory for Dalits and instructive to all non-Dalits in the caste-based, hierarchical context of India. He views the Samaritan as a Dalit (another brand of person who could not be used as a moral model in his own context) and comes to the following conclusion:

> The interesting thing in the parable is that both the marginalised Samaritan and the exploited traveller become one in their struggle to help each other. One oppressed person helps another. This gives us another important characteristic of Dalit theology. Dalit theology, if rightly understood, is not narrowly communal or sectarian. It does not seek to promote the liberation of Dalits alone thereby putting the non-Dalits out of the pale of God's salvation. Rather it seeks to challenge the tendency to legitimise cast oppression of Dalits.
> (Gnanavaram 1993:82)

Dalit hermeneutical strategy is both experiential and multi-modal, involving the senses and physical body in dance, drumming, painting and weaving. Akin to the Solentiname peasants who produced artistic representations for biblical reflection on their contemporary situation, for the Dalits, the Bible is not meant for flat dogma or moralism but rather a dynamic symbol that can dramatize liberation.

The gospel in the West

While one of the great contributions of Latin American, African and Indian folk interpretations has been to listen to contextual voices that had previously not been given a forum to express themselves, one of the great pities has been that these voices have time and again been pitted against mythical Western 'context-less scholars'. Pablo Richard tellingly believes that 'behind the scholars of the First World, there is a library. Behind the scholars of the Third World there are continents of poor and marginalized peoples' (Richard 2004:338). The strict division set up between community and folk readings and the so-called 'scholarly' readings of the West masks a fallacy. For all these readings are themselves 'context-full' of particular ideological perspectives (gender, race, power) or Eurocentric suppositions.

While many Western readings are explicit in proclaiming their 'reading agendas' (liberation, feminist, ecological etc.), still very few of these readings, within the West, are informed by work within local communities on the ground. The majority *modus operandi* of the Western exegete is still dialoguing with printed texts, not people in their own environments. Randall Bailey, in a critical review of the *Global Bible Commentary*, chastised the editors particularly on this point. He provocatively asks:

> What would happen to a reading of Genesis from the standpoint of the Brits who saw God having given them dominion over all and the imperative to subdue the whole land? I guess I am wondering if this approach to contextuality is within the framework that it is only the darker people who are contextual. Is this colonization of knowledge? . . . We have to ask, when will the 'white voice' become contextualized and put on the level playing field with the other contextual voices?
>
> (Bailey 2004)

Bailey is right to berate the length of time it has taken for folk readings to be employed in the Western world and make an impact on the academy, though contextual reading is of course as relevant in communities of the developed world as it is in the developing world. Ched Myers wagers that Western socialization trains readers to be passive spectators hugely reliant on so-called 'experts' – 'from plumbers to politicians' (Myers 2006:33) or, in biblical studies, priests and professors. This for Myers has done a disservice in the harvesting of potential meanings from the biblical texts within community contexts. Where such readings have been initiated, in Myers' opinion,

> Women, ethnic communities and churches of the poor have offered readings that not only reveal facets of scripture that white male academics and clerics could never see, but that also unmask the hidden interpretative interests of those professional classes.
>
> (Myers 2006:35)

In Britain the Contextual Bible Study movement recently set up a cell to work in Glasgow, Scotland. The religious sectarianism (which expresses itself more often in football team allegiance than religious discourse) and urban poverty that mark life in parts of Glasgow have contributed to some remarkable exchanges in this programme.

In such a context the text itself is made the unifying force, when denominational allegiance is perceived to divide participants. John Riches reports on two Contextual Bible Study groups, one parish based and another among students at Glasgow University, on the parable of the ten virgins. Both groups read the passage in light of the 'Make Poverty History Campaign', as Scotland prepared to host the G8 summit. He writes: 'the urgency of the parable is a call to action, and there are signs of new hope and belief that we can make a difference today, if not now, when?' (Riches 2005:25). Alison Peden facilitated a group at Cornton Vale Women's Prison in Stirling. Strong bonds of trust formed within the group; members had to formally accept new recruits before entry was permitted. No notes were taken at the sessions because inmates were suspicious of such documentation. The sessions were therefore viewed as an open arena, a safe space, in which they could express their innermost thoughts without any threat of comeback. Many of the women commented on the emotions of Jesus in the Garden of Gethsemane at his arrest. One reflected on her own arrest as 'emotionless' due to her being 'high on drugs'. She felt that emotions about the event were only starting to emerge now. Others reflected on Luke's infancy narratives and the plight of Mary and Elizabeth, both bearing sons that were to eventually leave their mothers. The prisoners directly translated these narratives into their own experiences of their children 'leaving' them, whether that was through them being taken into care, running away, or other means. They also talked critically about God's use of wombs. Peden writes: 'Many of these women have had their bodies used by others . . . they were not welcoming of a text which seemed to reduce women to only functional significance' (Peden 2005:17). The prisoners personalized the text from the outset. Like the Dalit readings outlined above, they saw that biblical narratives could give voice to their experience. The text was given profound correlation with their 'embodiment' and as such provided avenues to explore 'ways in which their lives may be transformed'.

A similar initiative has been undertaken by Bob Ekblad in the United States; his provocatively titled book *Reading the Bible with the Damned* (2005) captures 'marginal' perspectives of prisoners, immigrants and those subject to racial discrimination. He reminisces:

Reading Paul with undocumented immigrants and inmates invites us to a radical reorientation away from total allegiance to the state, denominations, and other principalities with their laws and doctrines, toward a 100 percent following after the One crucified outside the camp. Baptism into Christ's death as a lawbreaker is necessary if one is to effectively serve as a bearer of good news to people like Feliciano, Antonio, Andrew, Maria, Julio, Seferino, and any of today's undocumented immigrants and outlaws.   (Ekblad 2005:196)

Fernando Segovia and Mary Ann Tolbert's two-volume work, *Reading from this Place* (1995), also includes readings from diaspora communities and other marginal groups across Europe and North America.

John Vincent, founder of the Urban Theology Unit in Sheffield, has been a leading voice in so-called practice criticism in Britain. A recent volume edited by him, entitled *Mark: Gospel of Action*, provides some important material as regards British personal and community response to scripture: 'not just ways in which we use Mark's Gospel. It is ways in which Mark's Gospel uses us' (Vincent 2006:6). Tracing Mark in both 'Discipleship and Vocation' and in 'Community and Politics', the contributors variously trace the interface of the text with the contemporary contexts (even TV soap operas) in which it is used and read. The theology contained within these readings does not arise from the academic guild's interests, but rather the experiences and praxis (personal and political) of different reading groups. Vincent suggests a correlation between text and context born in action. In his words, 'We need not a repetition of the text, but a repetition of the kind of action that created the text – creative fidelity to the actions of Jesus' (2006:12). In this thinking, various interests and projects which fired Jesus and his movement (social inclusion, societal critique etc.) should act as catalysts for contemporary action reflecting that spirit. Building on Karl Barth's commentary on Romans and Clodovis Boff's liberation agenda, Christopher Rowland similarly outlines a related method of 'actualization' of the biblical text in the contemporary world, 'that is, reading of texts in light of new circumstances' (Rowland 2006a:5). Like Vincent, he is clear that scripture does not offer easy 'substance' that can be translated to contemporary situations, but it does provide illuminating pointers to the methodology that should underlie

Christian action today: 'not a *what* but a *how* – a manner, style, spirit' (Boff 1987, cited in Rowland 2006a:6).

The folk arts of biblical interpretation

This chapter has suggested that contextual interpretations prioritize the local folk consciousness of readers and encourage explicit engagement between texts and contexts of the present. In many areas across the world such approaches share a common identity with liberation readings (including an explicit emphasis on praxis as the outcome of interpretation). Folk biblical interpretations teach us that it is not just the 'scribal classes' of the biblical studies industry, but also the outcast, the peasant, the poor, to name but a few, that have important parts to play in the imagination of the 'word in place'. The diverse respondent groups each 'incarnate' the word anew in their own contexts and in turn open new vistas for others, to develop transforming ethical and theological perspectives.

Finally, a word on terminology: Gerald West has identified the 'ordinary reader' as referring to those at the margins of society in general and scholarly discourse in particular. Some have voiced dissent about the term and West's most recent work has identified 'extra-ordinary' African agency in some contextual readings (2007a:29–47). Stephen Jennings, while voicing misgivings about the prejudicial connotations involved in the term 'ordinary reader', nevertheless chooses to retain it within his work, for its power to convey one's social location (Jennings 2007:49). Throughout this chapter I have specifically avoided the term 'ordinary' reader and preferred 'folk' reader to demonstrate and celebrate the community consciousness and experience of those interpreters. In this project I have learned as much from folk readers as scholarly books and journals, and picture these pursuits as mutually enriching not mutually exclusive. Jonathan Boyarin offers a wonderful image of scholar and folk artist together in his ethnographic study of Jewish reading practice. He cites Rabbi Akiba Eger's vision of the messianic age where all the righteous sit down and study together. Boyarin submits:

> the point of the image is equidistance and equal view of one another:
> I can see your truth and you can see my truth. A related image is that

of the Tablets of the Law, which, the midrash asserts, were legible from all sides: truth can be seen from every perspective.

(Boyarin 1989:415)

In other words, polyphonic voices from past and present and different environments are heard together on equal terms.

The strength of employing the folk arts of biblical interpretation is that it can better serve to image not only the present local environment and world-view but also the past experiences contained in scripture and a future aligned with this. Folk readings not only unlock what people know, but also how they know and how they can re-imagine, and in so doing serve both to reinvigorate and to transform contexts and 'place' in their immediate locality and beyond.

3

Reading in place:
approaches and methods

A fresh look at the Bible suggests that a sense of place is a primary category of faith.

Walter Brueggemann

The gospel must be culturally contextualized, yet it must 'gospelize' the cultural context itself. The incarnation is the ultimate event of contextualization.

Shoki Coe

Contextual Bible Study is a place-making activity: it encourages communal and face-to-face sharing of stories in conjunction with biblical texts. Picking up on the place-making pointers outlined in Chapter 1, contextual readings encourage the development of justice, compassion and wisdom and as such offer 'homecoming' or 'place-making' opportunities. The fieldwork for this project utilized two main methodological perspectives: first, themed Contextual Bible Studies, and, second, ethnography of groups. The latter method initially strikes one as most helpful for clergy who are, in a sense, like an ethnographer, both insider and outsider to the communities they serve (for further discussion on clerical identity, see Chapter 8). However, even facilitators of Contextual Bible Studies who are themselves 'ordinary' members of the community will find the process of collective reflection on the nature of the group they inhabit a crucial exercise for theological reflection on context. With these thoughts in mind, this chapter aims to offer practical resources for the adoption of a 'reading in place' in a variety of contexts and contribute to what I have termed the construction of 'a hermeneutics of presence' (interpretation centred on 'being with' others), for reading with 'someone' 'somewhere' is inevitably an empathetic and creative pursuit.

Contextual Bible Study

As described in Chapter 2, Contextual Bible Study privileges folk consciousness responses to biblical texts and holds praxis as a key aim of interpretation. It begins by harvesting first impressions of a biblical story then encouraging readers to draw connections between a theme and context within the story and their own locality and contemporary concerns. Hampaté Ba's famed dictum that when a person is dying in Africa 'a library is on fire' (cited in Augé 1995:9) illustrates the profound importance of personal stories and experiences and what an intense loss to the community these are when they are not shared. Contextual Bible Study itself encourages the sharing of personal and experiential wisdom and, as such, shares common features with the pursuit of oral history. Oral history has also encouraged voices that have often been muted in the annals of 'official' history. The method's central component is a 'history built around people'. In Paul Thompson's words, 'it brings history into, and out of, the community . . . it makes for contact – and thence understanding between social classes and between generations. And to individual historians and others, with shared meanings, it can give a sense of belonging to a place or in time' (Thompson 2000:24). The sharing of oral histories has also been seen as important in pedagogical arenas in allowing voices not represented in dominant histories to be heard. Tineke Abma, in her article 'Learning by Telling', sees the dialogic process of storytelling as one in which discrete experiences and stories can relate to one another and collaboratively (re)create meaning (2003:223). In my work, as will be seen, I augmented the Contextual Bible Study process with a number of group activities. Many of the activities (including mapping) were inspired by Common Ground, an arts and environmental organization. Their website is worth consulting for more 'place-making' group tasks and ideas (<www.commonground.org.uk>). One of the great insights of the Common Ground initiative has been to disengage a sense of place from the purely 'chronological' in favour of a 'spatial' perspective. The spatial is more inclusive of all newcomers to an area, or, in theological terms, spatiality posits the entire context as a 'temple-like place of divine encounter' (Cameron *et al.* 2005:185).

It should be noted at the outset that ideally it would have been most fruitful to read an entire Gospel contextually with each group.

Much of our consumption of biblical texts within worship contexts is fragmented and loses the flow of the plot of the entire book in the process. However, given time constraints, I had to be more specific in my choice of texts in reference to the place themes outlined below. I decided to select texts from one single Gospel, Luke, in order to allow the groups to inhabit one text as far as was possible. The Lucan texts selected purposively represented a diversity of genres (parable; narrative and sayings etc.) and different christological images (boy, sage and miracle worker). This was also intentional, as part of my research involved tracing how different types of biblical texts were contextualized by the contemporary communities. I will return to the question of how these differences impacted on the contextual process in my hermeneutical reflections in Chapter 9. The main selection criteria for the texts and their specific ordering within the Contextual Bible Study process was patterned on specific place-related themes and issues. Figure 3.1 shows how these can be diagrammatically presented.

As the diagram illustrates, the 'place themes' are interrelated; none could be considered in entire isolation from another. That said, however, the sequence in which the texts and themes were

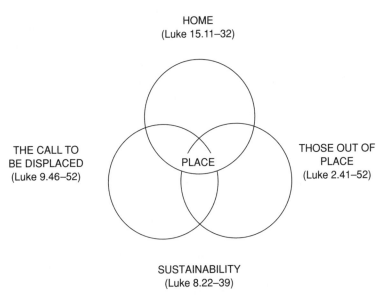

Figure 3.1 Place 'themes' and biblical texts

encountered by the contemporary communities in this project was strategic. The first theme considered in relation to place was 'home'. Tim Cresswell identifies this as 'the most familiar example of place' and 'a kind of metaphor for place in general' (2004:24). To experience the primal idea of 'dwelling somewhere' is in effect to encounter a concept of home. The parable of the lost son (Luke 15.11–32), the story selected in reference to the theme of home, provides a powerful stimulant to think through issues not only of home and journeys away from it, but also more importantly the nature of homecoming possibilities. The second theme, those out of place, is related to the first. Namely, this focuses on those individuals who do not occupy, spatially or ideologically, the idea of home. This theme starts to probe political, social and ideological maps of power which exclude certain individuals from certain places. Race, age, class, gender and sexuality can mark people as 'out of place' in one sense or another and as a result identify them as 'transgressors' of the dominant maps of meaning operative within a place (see Cresswell 1996). The biblical text chosen to illustrate this theme was Luke 2.41–45, the account of the boy Jesus in the temple. Here we have dominant maps of power and authority imaged in the temple authorities and teachers, being, in part, transgressed by a child who asks discerning questions and offers wisdom far beyond his age.

The third theme of 'sustainability of places' focuses on the threats to place and home encountered within our contemporary contexts, from environmental catastrophe to political or social oppression. The biblical story selected in reference to this theme was Luke 8.22–39, the stilling of the storm and the exorcism of Legion. This narrative provides evocative imagery to consider the various tempestuous seas that contemporary communities navigate, and through Legion consider the divided and fragmented personalities that various places may exhibit.

The final theme, the call to displacement, encourages communities to step out of their comfort zones and consider the ways in which dominating or 'static' ideas of place can stunt the development of authentic and inclusive visions for the future. The biblical passage chosen to stimulate reflection on this theme was Luke 9.46–52, sayings which encourage individuals to leave the known and familiar, and, as displaced itinerants, encounter the divine and build the Kingdom in other places.

Groups opted either to cover the place-related Contextual Bible Studies over four separate sessions or alternatively a single workshop day. The biblical stories were printed out on separate pages as stories, with chapter and verse notations removed. As some of the participants of the groups I worked with were non-Christian, each session was prefaced with the proviso that we were going to read an ancient text that contained wisdom regarding place-making. Each group was encouraged to sit in a circle. An ice-breaker activity was then given (details of these activities are listed below). Following this, I invited a volunteer from each group to read the story out loud. My role as facilitator (not leader or director) was primarily to ask the questions and encourage others to share their experiences and thoughts and listen to their own adoption of the 'word in place'. As with the multimodal approach of the Dalit and Nicaraguan peasants, some groups were encouraged to produce artistic and performative representations of their interpretations. At all times the local was contextualized in the global – or what recent theorists have called 'glocalism': 'the wider social nexus [which] impacts in material ways upon the lives of communities' (Graham, Walton and Ward 2005:225). More detailed introduction to the place themes are presented below, as are Contextual Bible Study materials on the respective biblical passages which were used in the fieldwork.

Theme 1: home

'Home alone' is an oxymoron (Bouma-Prediger and Walsh 2008:xi), for home is at base a collective enterprise. The growth of non-place in Western society can be read as a metaphor of 'homelessness', 'a matter of placelessness' (Bouma-Prediger and Walsh 2008:4). Migrancy and rootlessness means for the most part we are 'home dispensers', suffering from corporate amnesia about our stories of place and identity.

Bouma-Prediger and Walsh offer a number of different touchstones for 'thinking with home' and developing homemaking possibilities. They contend that home is a dwelling place, constituting relationships. This is what makes the difference between a mere house and a home. Home is also a place of shelter and is intimately related to the Christian virtue of hospitality, a practice that Christine Pohl (1999) suggests involves 'making room' and providing a 'safe place' for the needy. Home also is a place of particularity: it has particular smells, sounds and looks. Finally, home is 'a place of affiliation and belonging' (Bouma-Prediger and Walsh 2008:66) in which memories and experiences are shared and known and emotional and spiritual fulfilment can be found. Sheldrake likewise defines 'home' not just as a place where we are born, were raised, or inhabit, but rather any truly inhabited space that cultivates a sense of belonging. With this in mind Brown submits that one of those areas outside traditional sacred space that deserves serious theological reflection is home: 'there is a need to focus on the home once more as a place of sacramentality that can complement church in providing a sense of God's presence and care for his people' (Brown 2004:349). Despite the power of the image, many recent critics have questioned the idea of 'home' as unity. Feminists for instance have unmasked homes as gendered 'places of drudgery, abuse and neglect' (Rose 1993:56). Thus 'home' can be emblematic of fragmentation as well as unity according to the context.

'Home' and 'homecoming' stories are central in the biblical witness. The Exodus tradition plots out the founding of a home for the people of Israel and posits the 'homemaking creator' 'who insists that the people be set free' (Bouma-Prediger and Walsh 2008:16). Exile and return allegorizes Israel's apostasy and repentance as a homecoming, a bounded 'landedness' from radical 'landlessness' (Bouma-Prediger and Walsh 2008:21). Halvor Moxnes has recently shown how Jesus' ministry also questions versions of normality and power centred on place and more frequently emphasizes 'home' than 'cultic centres'. Moxnes builds upon those studies that have developed the contrast between regional extractive urban centres, such as Jerusalem and rural peasantry areas under Herodian control such as Galilee (Malbon 1986), to posit Jesus as someone who 'queers' traditional conceptions of religious space. He sees Jesus withdrawing from synagogue space to the market places, seashores, mountaintops and other liminal areas to imagine the Kingdom anew. Similarly in meal practice, exorcisms and healings the 'homecoming' practices of the Kingdom of God as opposed to the kingdoms of the world were exhibited and imagined differently (Moxnes 2003:254). In early Christianity the Church is purposively modelled on the 'household of God' and 'the body of Christ' to promote an economy of equality and interdependence. Moreover the Christian community is seen as God's dwelling place (1 Cor. 3.16–17) and linked through the story of his death and resurrection as fictive kin. The eschatological realm is also frequently envisioned as a home. John's Jesus promises his followers a room in his Father's house, which he will go and prepare for them (John 14.1–4).

Of course one of the most prominent stories of homecoming within the New Testament is the parable of the lost son (Luke 15.11–32) and it is this text that I chose to read in the Contextual Bible Study process. This is a story about leaving home, seeking fortune, property and wealth. But it is also a story about abundant homecoming: the father embraces his son, offers gifts and hosts elaborate festivities. It is also a story that contains unresolved conflict imaged in the elder son's negative evaluation of his brother. The Contextual Bible Study on this text is presented below as 'Contextual Bible Study 1'.

Contextual Bible Study 1: home (Luke 15.11–32)

Activities

Share with the group individual stories and memories of 'place' (variously understood as geographical, vocational or experiential according to the nature of the group) which people have in common. Perhaps ask people to bring along an object, artefact or picture of their choice that sums up their place and/or community, then get others to comment on the object. This can be insightful. For example, for one person a picture of a field can denote livelihood; for another an exploitable resource; for another a leisure pursuit; and for another a spiritual place (see Blewitt 2005:73).

Share your diverse experiences of place. Spell out the name of your place and for each letter think up all aspects of the place that you value (this can be anything from a part of the natural world to a tradition, to something seemingly trivial, for example a post box!).

Read Luke 15.11–32 and consider the following questions

- What immediately jumps off the page at you? This can be anything from an observation to a question.

- How do home and journeying feature in this story? Do any connections occur to you with life in your place?
- What parts do property and wealth represent in this story? Do they find any resonance in your context?

Theme 2: those 'out of place'

Mary Douglas first articulated the insight that 'dirt was matter out of place' (1966). She saw that various maps of meaning ordered the world and rendered some elements as 'unclean': a female in a male court, a corpse in the realm of the living and the 'unclean' in the 'holy' temple. To transgress these powerful maps of meaning was to risk being rejected and labelled as 'out of place' in one sense or another. Erving Goffman (1963) in a similar vein posited 'stigmatization' as a tool used by the powerful to 'dis-identify' with particular individuals on account of their disconnection from the dominant social order. Stigma in this respect was not something that an individual inherently had within their being, but rather a nexus of social conventions projected onto an individual. Tim Cresswell (1996) likewise notes that in those instances when cultural maps of meaning are not observed, a 'transgression', a crossing of a line, is deemed to have taken place. He uses the example of gypsies and New Age travellers 'disrupting' the serene habitus of the English countryside. He also notes that the more robust the spatial classification at work, the greater the desire will be to censor, expel, stigmatize and exclude. Groups that have been labelled in this way include people with mental health problems, political protesters, non-whites, gays, lesbians and bisexuals, prostitutes, the disabled, refugees, asylum-seekers, and all those who can be placed under the rubric of 'otherness' or 'abnormal' in a culture's maps of order. All those who potentially 'disturb the heteronormative character of many of the places that surround us' (Cresswell 2004:122) are in essence 'out of place'. Such 'depersonalizing' labels can be compared with the construction of 'social exclusion' as a trope in recent governmental rhetoric, denoting 'individuals from areas [which] suffer from a combination of linked problems such as unemployment, poor skills, low incomes, poor housing, high crime environments' (*Social Exclusion Unit Pack* 1997, cited in Cooper 2001:77). However, as Stephen Winter submits, in constructions of social exclusion as an impersonal problem the part society plays in such labelling is masked. He pleads for such debates to be earthed in human relationships, for in his words 'healing and the creation of inclusive societies requires a process of reconciliation' (Winter 2001:67) and reconciliation is only ever developed in real bonds between people, and the recognition of the parts each individual can play in the fragmentation or unifying of sectors in society.

Jesus' ministry has often been characterized as a 'boundary crossing' endeavour. The sick, the bleeding, the dead, life's nuisances and misfits are all reached out to and touched by him. The dominant maps of Jewish purity are 'transgressed' and to those that society marked as 'matter out of place' he offers a homecoming. Paul likewise constructs the body of Christ without hierarchical, racial or sexual divisions (Gal. 3.28); the religious maps of Judaism are redrawn by new Christian 'inclusive' cartography. In a culture that venerated age, ironically little children, life's least, become potent symbols of discipleship. Moxnes also sees this as an act of reversal that queers traditional and dominant expectations: 'in an act of reversal the Kingdom is ascribed not to adults but to children ... spatial hierarchies are turned upside down' (Moxnes 2003:92–3). For the Contextual Bible Study on 'those out of place', therefore, the story of the young Jesus in the temple (Luke 2.41–52) teaching a startled scribal class about the scriptures seems a provocative starting point to reflect on how one's maps of order can be unexpectedly contravened and dramatically redrawn as a result. The Contextual Bible Study on this theme can be planned as shown in the section below: 'Contextual Bible Study 2'.

Contextual Bible Study 2: those 'out of place' (Luke 2.41–52)

Activities

Get a number of copies of maps (ideally one for each participant) of your place (anything from Ordnance Survey maps to tourist maps will be fine). Maps are themselves tools of power; some people's stories are represented, other people's are not (see Clifford 1996:3–14). In one colour pen ask every individual to trace on the map the places they go on a day-to-day level; in a different colour ask them to mark places which they feel are sacred; in another colour again mark places of contest, conflict or dispute. Share and discuss the maps and markings together as a group.

Walk around the area, noting emotions, taking pictures etc., for use in collective reflection. Walking itself 'makes places': 'Pedestrians make cities their own place not by following the cartographer's map but in the improvised act of window shopping or strolling' (Cameron *et al.* 2005:180).

Collectively make a map (this need not be to scale or even follow conventional map-making tools; you may for example make it in the shape of a being or building). The map would seek to illustrate and tell the story of communal identity and perhaps redraw boundary lines within your place.

Read Luke 2.41–52 and consider the following questions

- What are your first reactions to this story?
- The story presents the family going to the city of Jerusalem to celebrate Passover. What rituals/celebrations/activities are celebrated in your place? Have these changed over the years? If so, why?
- In this story Jesus turns up in an unexpected place. Who is, or is treated as, 'out of place' in your context and who brings the unexpected?

Theme 3: sustainability

In the New Testament period, the imperial power of Rome threatened the sustainability and integrity of particular places. The imperial machine promulgated its own stories and myths that sought to overcome indigenous ways of life. Wes Howard-Brook and Anthony Gwyther's *Unveiling Empire: Reading Revelation Then and Now* (2001), for example, reveals how Rome's empire is set against God's Kingdom, how the Pax Romana is exposed as 'peace with a price' by the image of Babylon drunk on the blood of martyrs (Rev. 17.6). The story of Rome's eternity is pitted against the dissolution of Rome and the participants of the Kingdom of God reigning for ever (Rev. 22.5). Similarly, William Cavanaugh, in his celebrated work *Torture and Eucharist: Theology, Politics and the Body of Christ* (1998), writing on the Pinochet administration in Chile, saw the destructive

mythologies of 'torture' by the oppressive regime being deconstructed in a eucharistic 'counter-politics', a story which united rather
than tore apart communities. In our own era, global capitalism has
promoted stories (the media tells the truth; the accumulation of
personal wealth ensures happiness etc.) that have been damaging.
Exploitative economies have threatened the sustainability of local
businesses and agriculture. Poverty has grown like a cancer among
certain sectors of society and an economics of scarcity rather than
generosity has threatened the potential flourishing of many. As I
write this, there is a global financial crisis afoot; has the greed of
financial markets finally come home to roost in the 'credit crunch'?
In an age of ecological crisis the 'sustainability' of planet earth has
also been put firmly on our agenda. Human impact on the natural
world has reaped grim harvests: global warming, soil degradation,
loss of forests, loss of natural habitats and biodiversity.

One particularly evocative biblical story on the theme of sustainability is the stilling of the storm and the exorcism of Legion (Luke
8.22–39). The storm narrative has fear for one's life at its heart, the
boat providing a powerful image of community in crisis. The Legion
narrative presents a multiple personality that is fragmented and
self-destructive: indeed many have read the name as 'double-voiced',
referring to Rome's military occupation of land. Moxnes similarly
reads exorcisms 'spatially' and views shamanic activities as powerful forms of resistance to colonial oppression. He sees locative categories at the heart of cosmological battles: 'the image of the realm of
Satan in opposition to the realm of God . . . The exorcism represented
a form of power "from below" that was a challenge to established
authorities' (Moxnes 2003:140). Robert Tannehill, in his commentary
on the third Gospel, tells us how Luke's original readers may have
conceived of their own conversion to Christianity as a release from
'demons' or more specifically idols and pagan gods. He writes:

> the more strident label of demons is dangerous, but there is a sense
> in which gods possess their worshipers, sometimes with destructive
> consequences; this story then could both represent individual con-
> versions and be a sign of hope for the purging of demons from pagan
> culture as a whole. (Tannehill 1996:148)

The passage seems to offer particularly powerful images to reflect
on in relation to the sustainability of communities and places. The

section below, 'Contextual Bible Study 3', shows what a session on this passage might look like.

> ## Contextual Bible Study 3: sustainability (Luke 8.22–39)
> ### Activities
>
> On a flipchart list 'strengths', 'weaknesses', 'opportunities' and 'threats' for the local community in your area.
>
> If you were part of the non-human world (animal, vegetable, mineral, built environment etc.), what would be your manifesto for the future?
>
> ### Read Luke 8.22–39 and consider the following questions
>
> - What are your first reactions to this story?
> - In these stories various elements are stirred up (the sea, people etc.). How do people in this place react to being stirred up? Do things/people get healed or do things/people get driven out?
> - Legion is often said to represent a land occupied by a foreign/colonial power (Rome). What threatens your place and land?
> - What action can be taken to liberate your place from the threats you have identified?

Theme 4: the call to be displaced

I have already hinted at the ways in which Western culture has 'displaced' people from their immediate location. Despite the previous emphasis on a construction of place and homecoming as an antidote to these trends, at the heart of the gospel message is a radical call from the familiarity of home, often to seemingly God-forsaken places, to encounter the divine. Displacement is a guard against too rigid a sense of place. Christians are called to be 'sojourners': 'the pilgrim knows that there is a "not yet" character to this indwelling; we are still sojourning toward that final homecoming, and thus we are not to erect any home this side of the eschaton as a fortress of finality' (Bouma-Prediger and Walsh 2008:296). Christians are not rooted so much in place, as the story and future hope of the biblical witness: 'Christian sojourners are people of the Book who love one another and entertain angels . . . [W]ithout biblical memory, generous community and sacrificial hospitality, no authentic Christian community can exist' (Bouma-Prediger and Walsh 2008:302).

Early Christian itinerancy also witnessed to the fact that the whole inhabited earth was the arena for the Kingdom of God to be proclaimed and realized. Jesus called followers to leave behind livelihoods, to 'leave the dead to bury the dead' and to follow the Kingdom (Luke 9.46–52). The 'son of man' had nowhere to lay his head and likewise those children of the Kingdom were to be displaced in the world's sense, 'stripped of that which defined their position and status' (Moxnes 2003:71) and called out to places far from home. The Kingdom sayings throughout Luke 9.46–52, which provide radical calls to leave behind one's place for the sake of the Kingdom, are provocative, literally 'unsettling', statements to reflect upon in this light. 'Contextual Bible Study 4' (below) gives an indication of what a discussion of Luke 9.46–52 might look like.

Contextual Bible Study 4: the call to be displaced (Luke 9.46–52)

Activities

If the group is of varying ages, make the youngest people put themselves into the shoes of the elderly and consider the three priorities they think the latter would want for community change. Then let the elderly identify three priorities for change that they imagine young people would want.

As a group, identify heroes and heroines of the community (these can be historical, living, fictional etc.). What was it about them, their story and their accomplishments that were so impressive for community and place-building? What can we learn from them today?

Read Luke 9.46–52 and consider the following questions

- What are your first impressions of this narrative?
- What do you make of the saying 'foxes have holes and birds of the air have nests but the Son of Man has nowhere to lay his head'?
- Is it good or bad to have a strong sense of home or place?
- 'Following' is a key theme in the context of this narrative. Who or what is 'followed' in your context?
- What is the urgent concern for the future of your place? What issue demands that everyone put their 'hands to the plough'?

Ethnography of groups

My role in this project was akin to an anthropologist who adopts a 'participant-observer' role within communities; this involves both outsider detachment (an etic perspective) and insider involvement (an emic perspective). In many ways this participant-observer role is precisely the position that clergy occupy in serving their communities: being both a member of those communities but also an outsider who can act as a commentator on the context. This is not to say, however, that collective self-reflection by communities on themselves is not a viable or useful exercise. Indeed many communities through such processes have been enabled to gain perspective on their situations and make plans for the future. This mode of ethnographic enquiry, in which insiders begin to reflect on their own collective identity, can be particularly enlightening and fruitful. Ethnographers who write about their own places and situations do so under the banner of 'auto-ethnography', a genre which often includes (like Contextual Bible Study) the sharing of personal stories. In short, for both clergy and lay person, insider and outsider, tools which allow one to start to read communities are absolutely central in promoting theological reflection on contexts. In refining my method I was profoundly influenced by Leonora Tubbs Tisdale's book *Preaching as Local Theology and Folk Art* (1997), which adopts an ethnographic perspective to 'exegete communities' alongside the 'exegesis of texts' and in effect constructs a Geertzian 'thick description' of communities.

Tubbs Tisdale's project asked the question, 'How does one go about reading the signs and symbols of congregational life in order to discern congregational world-view, values and ethos?' (1997:18). Despite the fact that Tubbs Tisdale's project was directed to congregations, I found it could easily be transferred to a wider variety of groups, including regional communities, villages etc. Continuing the social-scientific analogy, she outlines seven symbols for community exegesis that unlock the conceptual and material world of the subjects among whom one lives and works (1997:64–90). These can be summarized as follows:

- *Stories and interviews*. Storytelling by the community about their history and experiences tells a lot about their identity. Are there particular images or metaphors that could offer insight into community world-views? By interviewing a cross-section of the group, including those often not heard, one can also learn in different ways about important cultural beliefs, texts, histories and social change.

- *Archival materials.* Here official reports, records, pictures, artefacts, recordings, news bulletins and the like give an insight into the group's material 'culture'.
- *Demographics.* Profiles of a typical group member need to be produced and diversity detected within the group.
- *Architecture and visual arts.* The socio-contextual locations of the community communicate something of its identity, also its immediate buildings and place. Environments 'often bespeak either past or present . . . [and offer] clues to the ways in which a congregation [/group] participate in a larger plot' (1997:71).
- *Rituals.* Calendrical rites, critical rites, rites of solidarity and rites of passage all could be documented here.
- *Events and activities.* Here local cultural events deserve special attention. What activities demand most attention? Which are most controversial? Which events make this community unique among others in its environment?
- *People.* Who or what symbolize the values of the group? Who are considered mainstream and who are seen as extreme or 'out of place'?

Tubbs Tisdale reveals that the above methods offer plenty of raw data, but one has to dig a little deeper in order to start constructing the world-view(s) and ethos of various groups. Tubbs Tisdale gives us further help here in interpreting, in her words, 'congregational ethos' centred on categories of 'View of God', 'View of Humanity', 'View of the Church', 'View of Time', 'View of Christian Mission' and 'View of Creation'. Let us focus briefly on some questions posed by the 'View of Creation' as an example. Tubbs Tisdale offers two questions to probe. First, 'What is the understanding of creation and the place of human beings within it?' (1997:82). Is the basic stance towards nature one of harmony (as in farming communities where people live intimately with land) or 'mastery over the natural world', exhibited in certain built environments. Second, she asks, 'How would this group describe the manner in which human beings ought to live in relation to nature?' (1997:82). 'What interpretation of the meaning of human dominion in relation to creation is reflected in the signs and symbols of [group] life?' (1997:82).

Tools to facilitate the reading of communities (by both internal and external members), alongside the reading of texts, are crucial in any contextual endeavour. Tubbs Tisdale's work follows well-trodden pathways in congregational studies, which have long called for attention to the local and particular in order to communicate proficiently within communities. Akin to the ethnographer's reflections on fieldwork, in such studies the gap between the ideal picture of a community and the experienced reality can also be approached.

A hermeneutics of presence

The methodologies outlined above have as their main focus *engagement* with people and their experiences, stories and places. Gerald West reveals that such engagement 'is not contrary to critical understanding, but a component of it' (West 2004:76). Christopher Rowland likewise sees engagement with and among grass-roots communities as an important component of the critical task. He tells the story of a colleague at Oxford asking him the deceptively simple question of whether his attitude to scripture was one focused on 'inspection or reception' (Rowland 2000:26). Rowland understands this question to be, 'Does the text constitute a problem to be solved?' Can someone trained in the requisite language and historical context make the text 'less intractable, less wild, more acceptable and comprehensible to modern sensibilities' (Rowland 2000:27)? Of course, this sort of specialized reading does play an important part within the professional exegete's job description. However, it is also true that grass-roots readings of the Bible can yield surprising results and encourage the scholar to reappropriate, in Rowland's words, 'an attitude of humility rather than superiority before the text' (Rowland 2000:28). These types of contexts serve to make real and alive the links between the Bible and the world, and give the professional guild a sense of perspective on their own readings, and the modesty to acknowledge the profound insights that can come from folk voices.

'In-service' methodology, namely voluntary service which involves theological reflection, offers another set of important resources for imagining the word in place. This time, however, the engagement process does not directly encourage grass-roots readings of the Bible, but rather critical reflection by the individuals on the biblical texts in light of in-service experience. I adopted Alicia Batten's recent article 'Studying the Historical Jesus Through Service' (2005) to affirm that 'bias has heuristic value' (2005:108) in a New Testament module I recently taught. The method, however, could easily be transplanted into communities whose members were encouraged to undertake voluntary work within their contexts and collectively share their responses to their diverse experiences in reference to biblical narratives. Batten encouraged her students through service experiences to confront these biases and document any changes of perspective that had occurred as a result of their involvement. Batten's students went out into contexts as diverse as soup kitchens, shelters, hospices and residential homes, assigned with a fivefold task. First, they had to 'record what they observed at the site, including the physical surroundings, the interactions taking place, the smell and sounds' (2005:110), in as impartial terms as they could manage. Second, they were to confront their own prejudices: 'What pre-suppositions did they have? What were their actions? Why did they feel uncomfortable?' (2005:110). Third, students were asked to consider the immediate situations they found themselves in: 'What problems were people facing here … cultural, social, economic, physical, and/or linguistic?' (2005:110). Fourth, students had to link the particular problems or the individuals they encountered to structural/social causes concerning race, gender, disability, class and sexual orientation. Fifth, material obtained from the service experience had to be juxtaposed and read alongside material from the 'historical Jesus' module: 'What types of chronic injustices in first-century Palestine (for example, exploitative patronage, onerous taxation) were comparable to the injustices they witness today?' (2005:110). One student working in an AIDS hospice recognized the social isolation that this disease evoked and compared it with those ostracized in the first century on account of demon possession or leprosy. Another offering language lessons in a mixed community felt the fellowship within the group had mustered 'hope' among the participants, something she saw as central to the mission of Jesus. Some students felt that those among whom they worked did not appreciate their efforts. However, within this criticism lay another important lesson to be learned. As Batten reveals, citing a student journal, 'to truly serve one must reach out even when the response is uncertain because as Jesus said, "if you love those who love you what credit is that to you?" And then, the heart of service is radical and beautiful; it shows humanity at its best' (Batten 2005:110). Reflection on the social and structural causes of particular plights nudged students from a 'charitable giving' mindset and the concomitant risk it holds for masking 'our part' and 'role' in injustice and marginalization of others. Perhaps, as the in-service learning paradigm teaches, in order to avoid a certain 'domestication' of the text, we must recapture and expose ourselves to its 'alien' nature once more. One student on my module commented on how her experience of working in a refuge for street women had completely turned upside down her vision of stories surrounding such women in scripture. The student talked about her in-service learning experience 'de-sanitizing' the biblical pictures of beautiful and delicate prostitutes often featured in stained glass or romantic Bible illustrations.

Truly to embody a 'hermeneutics of presence' one must engage in people's lives and experience in all their social and religious diversity. The methods outlined in this chapter – Contextual Bible Study, participant observation and in-service learning – will I hope provide some practical tools to work towards this vision both for communities to reflect on their own identity and for those who seek to minister to them. For if 'scribes trained for the Kingdom of Heaven' do indeed bring treasures old and new from their store, then the results of 'reading in place' in folk contexts should be valued as new jewels among that treasure.

Part II

READING THE NEW TESTAMENT IN CONTEMPORARY CONTEXTS

4

Reading in a city

Designing a dream city is easy; rebuilding a living one takes imagination.

Jane Jacobs

The cityscape provides a very particular context in which to consider the 'word in place'. In Western thinking the city has featured not just as a physical place but also a mythological place. 'Cities of the mind' have come to represent both dystopia and utopia: 'Sodom, the city of corruption' and 'Athens, the city of enlightenment, democracy and reason' (see Bridge and Watson 2000:3). In the Bible likewise cities have frequently been used as places to 'imagine with'; moreover inhabitants of particular cities are frequently seen to share characteristics of their place. Babylon is representative of those cities that frustrate God's purposes and are invaded by forces of evil, disorder and disease (seen in political, social and cosmological descriptions). In marked contrast the Bible ends with a vision of new creation imaged as a city. This New Jerusalem is a 'utopian' community enjoying restored relationships between humanity, nature and God. The Christian is a citizen (and accordingly takes on characteristics) of 'Jerusalem above', always motivated by 'confidence in God's promise to establish his city' (Ryken *et al.* 1998:154) at the end of time. The ambivalent nature of city-space is also shown in Jesus' mission. He is more openly received in rural areas than city-space where he encounters fierce conflict and opposition and eventually a torturous death outside Jerusalem's walls. Early Christianity spread rapidly through urban space (Jerusalem, Antioch, Ephesus, Corinth and Rome etc.), but these cities became sites of persecution just as much as missionary promise.

Concretely defining a 'city' in both the ancient and contemporary worlds has not been an easy task. Gideon Sjoberg, in his work on pre-industrial cities, argued that the presence of a literate elite distinguished cities from other types of settlement (Blanton

1976:251). Eric Stewart notes that cities were conceived as 'civilized areas' in the ancient world: 'the presence of religious institutions distinguished these territories from those that surrounded them' (Stewart 2005:192). In contemporary analyses a city has been defined as a central place ('a large grouping of civic-ceremonial buildings and palaces') in the 'hierarchy of central places' (Blanton 1976:253). However, much recent urban anthropology has now retreated from macro-categorizations in favour of 'context-specific' approaches to urban realms, in effect reading cities as 'texts'. Following this line Graham Ward conceived of a city as a chronicle 'written by all those who walk down its streets, drive down its boulevards . . . and more generally, impact upon its mapped out body' (Ward 2000:4). Ultimately, however we choose to define these cityscapes is second to the realization that if one is to build 'places' that breathe shalom, one has to take seriously the urban realities, for good and ill, in which many live.

The city in theological reflection

The city has been the subject of intense theological reflection over the last 25 years. *Faith in the City* (1985) was an Anglican initiative that put social poverty and marginalization firmly on the theological agenda. The report, however, has been subject to criticism due to its unrealistic theological assertions in the social climate of the time. Some felt it was blind to the fact that social-atomism was so rife in the 1980s that mere language of collaboration and solidarity was meaningless in that era. It spoke of 'state' and 'nation' in a time of increasing globalization and posited the church as uniquely placed to cater for society's ills when 'the church [itself] albeit in a different way, is as marginal as so many of the poor it portrayed' (Ward 2000:28). While biblical principles underpinned many of the recommendations of the report, others have since pointed out that specific communal readings of scripture within cities (or indeed much praxis on the ground) was severely lacking: 'Using the terms of Carlos Mesters, there is a solid attention to the social context, the pre-text and also interest in encouraging communities to use participatory methods in order to empower people, *but the missing element is methodology in general and Bible reading methodology in particular*' (my italics, Latvus 2007:135).

The 1995 *God in the City* report (Sedgwick 1995) did pursue more earnestly base voices within cities. Spirituality was identified as an important element in community building but the large majority of the recommendations likewise brought worship and liturgy as opposed to Bible reading to the fore. In Kari Latvus's terms,

> the Bible may be recommended *to them* and may also be interpreted *for them*. Perhaps this doing-things-for-other-people tradition was stronger than the empowering trend in liberation theology. One further answer might be that the Anglican tradition in Britain is more concentrated on liturgy than on the word.
>
> (my italics, Latvus 2007:137)

The 2006 report, *Faithful Cities*, undertaken by the Commission on Urban Life and Faith, put forward as its central component the development of 'faithful capital'; the current climate is far more open to such terminology than it was 25 years ago, given the importance of religious belief and rhetoric in recent world affairs in our multicultural environments. 'Faithful capital' is seen to involve both language and praxis. Language that unites faiths is centred on stories involving justice, hope, forgiveness and hospitality. The commission saw that such stories have the ability to 'challenge dominant definitions in public policy' (2006:3). Praxis arising from 'faithful capital' involves people working together within a locality and recovering experiences of people in cities in order to construct 'everyday/ vernacular' theologies. The theological rationale for the report was, in large part, biblically based. Scripture tells us of the incarnation, itself a powerful image of Christ in the city: his rejection speaks powerfully of oppressive control and social exclusion; the theme of restlessness for mission reminds communities that while 'they need places to perform their rituals' they 'don't need to command or control space' (2006:57). The theme of (urban) regeneration is itself a biblical one, literally denoting 'being born again'. And finally the vision of the New Jerusalem informs action which works to accomplish God's will 'on earth as in heaven' (2006:67). The city as such is a place of encounter between people and God. It is a place 'between what is and what is to come. It is a place of waiting, but also the space in which humanity is called to work for God's purposes' (2006:54).

While the *Faithful Cities* report helpfully underlines the pursuit of 'faithful capital' on a ground level, it is once again notable that specific contextual readings of scripture are not outlined as important resources to enable Christian communities to reflect on, and collectively re-imagine for the future, the local urban environments in which they live. Such ground-level initiatives are an absolute priority given the individualistic 'non-places' that hallmark much of Western urban space. In Brown's words:

> Pluralism and transience with its accompanying lack of engagement with locality are thus undoubtedly two major inhibitors of history and story functioning as a means of mediating the divine in the modern city. It is thus perhaps here rather than in modern town planning . . . that the issue is at its most acute. It is to be noted though that the point is not that God is absent but rather human decision-making makes it more difficult to provide stimulants towards such experiences.
>
> (Brown 2004:188)

Addressing this lacuna and working towards the mobilization of local collective consciousness, here I will catalogue contextual readings gathered within an urban regeneration area in the city of Plymouth. As part of the regeneration plan, a spirituality audit, of the type recommended by the *Faithful Cities* report, was conducted. It provides a useful touchstone to supplement the contextual readings and reflect further on how urban regeneration can be informed by, and play a part in, shaping 'the word in place' through contextual biblical contemplation.

Introducing Plymouth

Plymouth is a city situated on the South Devon coast. It has a quarter of a million inhabitants and since the Industrial Revolution has been a major shipping port and centre for the Royal Navy. It suffered huge losses in the bombings of the Second World War and as a result much of the centre had to be virtually rebuilt. Patrick Abercrombie was the architect for the city's post-war redevelopment. His vision for the city centre was of wide-open avenues and a central boulevard that would link the railway station to Plymouth Hoe. The Abercrombie design for the rest of the city included settlements each equipped with central green spaces and community amenities. In essence the plan was a good one, but cheap building materials were used in the urban reconstruction and 60 years later much of the physical fabric is corroding and looking tired.

Currently Plymouth is once again undergoing redevelopment. Drake Circus shopping mall was opened to great acclaim in 2006; the shell of a church bombed in the blitz framing the new mall stands as a commemoration to those killed. The memory of the Second World War looms large in the built environment of the city; indeed it is estimated that there are 20 war memorials in the city centre. Government funding has also facilitated the redevelopment of particular pockets of social deprivation within the city. One such area lies by the dockyard, Devonport.

Devonport: ruin and regeneration

Jan Schneider and Ida Susser consider 'the mounting crises of con-temporary urban life' in their evocatively entitled work *Wounded Cities* (2003). The 'wounded' metaphor is a suggestive one, for it con-ceives of the city as a living, organic being, a 'body politic' which can be collectively injured or hurt, healed or renewed. Globalization and consumerist processes are seen to inflict certain sores on the bodies of our cities. These include pollution, social fragmentation, pros-titution, crime, addictions and fabric decay, all contributing to the rise of 'non-place'. In John Inge's words, 'cars, grime and graffiti turn places into dehumanising spaces (devoid of community and inter-action) . . . the manner in which they enrich people's humanity is lost' (Inge 2003:20). Other injuries include stark divisions between rich and poor, and the radical polarization of 'organs' of the city into the (plush) business district, the (privileged) residential suburb and the (poor) council estate.

In many respects Devonport can be seen to bear the urban scars outlined above. An area of social deprivation, it stands as a shadow of its former glory days. At one time it was home to the largest dockyard in Western Europe. In 1945, 21,000 people were employed there; figures for 1997, however, revealed this employment had been dramatically reduced to 3,500 (Gripaios, Gripaios and Munday 1997:583). Devonport's physical space also bears the scars of spatial fragmentation. In the 1950s the Ministry of Defence erected a wall around the original marketplace of the area to house a new Navy storage facility. Some locals have acrimoniously compared this to

Figure 4.1 The Devonport wall

the 'Berlin Wall'. The barely visible top of the original commercial centre and market hall behind the wall stood as potent insignia of the lost heart of the community. One could question ironically with David Delaney in his study of territorial space, 'if this is security . . . what [might] insecurity feel like?' (Delaney 2005:3).

Devonport has been identified as one of the 29 national priority areas for regeneration. A ten-year scheme for reconstruction funded by the New Deal for Communities programme to the tune of £48 million is currently in process in the area. The recent destruction of the wall itself became a powerful symbol of the rebirth of the place. Plans include housing and mixed-use neighbourhood facilities (healthcare, shops, offices). The market site in the formerly walled space will now be used once more as a central public square. Schneider and Susser caution, however, that within urban recovery plans lie further potential 'wounding' processes, by exposing a city very directly to 'neo-capitalist pressures'. They note how developers often 'target damaged locations' and 'transform the landscape into their own image' (rather than God's): 'a foremost and often over-riding goal is to generate profits for transnational corporate interests

associated with finance, name brand shopping, and tourism'
(Schneider and Susser 2003:4). In such developments cities market
themselves as commodities and this can lead to the eradication of
places of meeting between various classes and groups in favour of
'pristine new tourist and consumer-friendly zones', which may in
themselves 'mask a precipitous decline in social solidarity' (Schneider
and Susser 2003:4).

As an antidote to such 'depersonalizing' impulses, Patsy Healey
urges developers to see cities not as material or economic objects but
imaginary organisms capable of inclusive and collective acts (Healey
2002:1778). This sort of 'imagining' includes, in her opinion, listening to the everyday experience of inhabitants as well as considering economic and environmental perspectives. For 'the city is to be
more than merely some kind of backcloth, or symbolic painting that
hangs ignored in the arenas of organisational life of city administra-
tors, it thus has to be brought to life, to become an active performer
in the city which it is taken to represent' (Healey 2002:1782). In some
way, taking heed of this aspiration was the presence of an explicitly
spiritual component within the regeneration plan for Devonport.
Pre-empting many of the recommendations of the *Faithful Cities*
report, the Faith and Quality of Life Strategy (a report that considered urban regeneration from an explicitly faith-based perspective)
developed specific plans to nurture and use 'faithful capital' within
the Devonport restoration project: faith and quality of life denoting
'all faiths and faith in human beings'. In reality the majority of
reflections are Christian, but this is perhaps not surprising given
recent census figures which estimated around three-quarters of the
population of the entire city are Christian and eight churches are the
sole worship sites listed in the Strategy for the immediate area. For
the purposes of the Faith and Quality of Life Strategy (FQLS), 'faith'
was defined in as broad a sense as possible as

> a belief or trust in something or someone beyond us and within us
> that may or may not be expressed in traditional religious terms. This
> may result in shared relationships with others whether in small group
> settings or in a larger community one.
>
> (Nixon and Mawhinney 2005)

The FQLS also outlined that static targets and outcomes, so often
the genre of government objectives, were too blunt. Rather, faith and

quality of life demanded an organic nurturing of processes and people. Thus quality of life was defined in the FQLS as 'personal satisfaction or dissatisfaction with the culture or intellectual conditions under which you live (as distinct from material comfort)' (Nixon and Mawhinney 2005).

The FQLS focus group undertook a small-scale spiritual audit consisting of interviews with thirty-two persons in seven groups, three related to faith communities and four to secular community groups. David Nixon, chair of the group and co-author of the resultant report, explicitly outlined their aims as first an 'increase in faith communities' involvement in regeneration of Devonport'; second, an 'increase in people's expressed spiritual, emotional and mental well-being'; and third, an 'increase in self-esteem and confidence across the community' (Nixon and Mawhinney 2005).

Many stark voices from the ground were recorded in the consultancy process. To one young man, the image of God was itself a source of hurt, for he experienced fear and danger as part of his daily life. Others focused on the fact that 'if God exists he is sick', to illustrate what they perceived as the 'conflict-ridden nature of religion' (Nixon and Mawhinney 2005). More positive comments, though, revealed how local inhabitants concretely linked physical regeneration with a sense of spiritual regeneration; one participant triumphantly declared, 'God is alive and lives in Granby Way' (Nixon and Mawhinney 2005). One of the central recommendations of the FQLS was the importance of constructing communal stories in which all could partake. Nixon and Mawhinney reveal that many of those interviewed felt they 'had lost their place in the story and have difficulty refinding it, or even deciding what the story is'. Only 4.5 per cent of Devonport residents felt they had a measure of control over their lives and could make a difference in the community, compared to 15 per cent in Plymouth as a whole (Nixon and Mawhinney 2005). All in all the Devonport audit came to similar conclusions to the *Faithful Cities* initiative, namely that religious or faithful capital needed to be nurtured and developed and stories from all sectors of the area needed to be heard. A subtext was that the area should be conceived as an organic and living community that promoted collective values and fostered powerful social relationships founded on authentic engagement.

Contextual readings from Devonport

I worked with a small church group (15 people) and met in Stoke Damerel Parish Church, a building that has been the site of Christian worship for more than 700 years. Although this parish centre is not physically in the regeneration area, it is very close by and most participants in the group lived and worked within the regeneration area.

We began with people sharing their own experiences of their place. Physical urban wounds that were identified in the group included dilapidated flats, unsightly derelict land, rubbish in communal passageways and dog mess on the streets. Less physical urban 'wounds' included the fact that many did not feel safe at night and the place no longer had a sense of celebration surrounding important historical or religious events. Also, common virtues did not seem to be collectively pursued: it was only negative experiences that linked people – debt, crime (as perpetrators and victims), widespread substance addiction and family break-up.

We started by considering the themes of 'home and journeying' in relation to the lost son narrative (Luke 15.11–32). From the outset it was quite striking how the participants portrayed the 'homelessness' of Devonport, or rather the 'fragmentation' of home, witnessed there. All the participants agreed that the place where the younger son went to waste his inheritance in dissolute living struck more chords with their wider area than the father's house and farm. Comments included: 'dissolute living is only a few streets away'; 'the unclean pigs are in Plymouth'; 'it is an alien world with different cultural values than the church wants to promote'. These comments struck a particular chord in relation to the sex industry in certain pockets of Plymouth. The image of prostitution at the end of the story, so common in biblical thinking to illustrate apostasy (Hos. 4.12; Jer. 2.20), was picked up on by one participant as a distinct example of values that contradict the values of the Kingdom of God. It is also perhaps no coincidence that many ancient people believed that places could contain one's essence or personality (see Stewart 2005:40). In Devonport, similarly, it seems that the nature of the 'home' in the biblical story was far from the perceived 'personality' of their place. It is perhaps not unrelated that the 'far country' terminology within the story, which they identified with more easily, powerfully illustrates places still far from embodying the ideal of 'home'.

One particularly arresting comment in relation to these themes was the observation that the younger son within the biblical story did not feel the complete desperation of many in their city: 'He has a job at least, even if it is feeding swine!' This is quite a different reading of the image than the one usually forwarded by historical-critical scholarship that underlines the uncleanliness of pigs and their symbolic status within Jewish thinking of 'filth and paganism'. Leland Ryken *et al.* suggest that the prodigal was no doubt horrified to be reduced to feeding pigs, 'but it was worse to covet their food, the very source of their uncleanness' (Ryken *et al.* 1998:29). The group also commented on the fact that complete desperation is not evident in the story, for the son did not take his own life; rather, he still felt there was a place to go back to, home had not been irrevocably dispensed with. Many others commented in this connection on the recent high-profile drug-related death of a boy at the local school.

All participants realized that the 'homecoming' reception of hospitality, affiliation and belonging was a central image for them to build upon in conceiving of the word in their place. They saw that one had to think outside the traditional walls of the sacred, to work alongside the community. The costliness and risk of reaching out to the city prodigals, often smeared with 'stinking pig mess' on their persons, whether through occupation, addiction, prostitution or abuse, was also discussed. One participant who was a volunteer within a charity that provided refuge for 'working girls' was able to share the warmth and friendliness of the girls to other members of the group, offering an interpretation based on 'being with' individuals in a community which conveyed something of the person behind the stereotypical stigmatizing label. The work of Twelve's Company, first set up in 1985 in Devonport as a café and meeting place sponsored by the Church Urban Fund and Exeter Diocese, was also seen as part of the 'homemaking' project, promoting the gathering of 'alternative' stories of healing and reconstruction. The Company's mission statement is 'To enable and empower families, individuals and groups to take action on health, education and training and work which improves the quality of personal and community life, physically, mentally and spiritually' (see <www.twelvescompany.co.uk>). Its recent work among youth and counselling of victims of sexual violence (although its base has since moved from Devonport) was seen to provide something akin to the homecoming welcome by the father in the story.

Moving on to the theme of 'those out of place' and considering the story of the boy in the temple in Luke 2.41–52, it was instructive that some members of the group linked the image of the boy with adolescents within their own community. Those who worked alongside youth groups commented on the surprising 'generational revelation' that could come from such exchanges. Others spoke about how the church itself perhaps spoke a language that youth culture at large did not understand. One therefore needed, as the spirituality audit in the area had revealed, to 'experience' and work alongside young people, prizing relationships with them above preconceived 'intuitive' impressions.

Reflecting on the stilling of the storm and the exorcism of Legion narrative (Luke 8.22–39) in relation to sustainability, the group again offered some unexpected contextual reflections. The church as a boat was an evocative image. One participant noted that their church was expanded in the eighteenth century to deal with the influx of personnel from the Navy at the dockyard. The participant told me that according to tradition the Admiralty had sponsored part of this construction by giving parts of ships to be used as building materials and offering free labour from the dockyard workers. The 'journey to the other side of the lake' also brought powerful images to mind of the great explorers and Pilgrim Fathers who had left Plymouth's shores to find new worlds. Plymouth celebrated these figures, along with Sir Francis Drake, of Spanish Armada fame. This history is powerfully 'inscribed' within the city in name (Armada Way, Drake Circus etc.), not least for the tourist trade around the Hoe and Barbican, so it is perhaps no coincidence that these memories seemed strong 'stories' for the group to remember collectively.

The peril at sea experienced by the disciples in the biblical narrative led to reflections on the perils of the 'land' in Plymouth. Again picking up on a dominant historical theme it was noted how Plymouth sided with the Parliamentarians in the Civil War and as such the Royal Citadel had cannons pointing towards the city, as a warning to the potential rebels there. In some respects, therefore, participants within the group 'personalized' the city as a resistant place. 'Powers from below' could effect change. This gave an interesting interpretation of the exorcism narrative that many have read as a 'locative' story, emphasizing resistance to oppression. The threats of social fragmentation were again rehearsed in relation to the multiple personalities of Legion. The fact that Legion was instructed to 'go home' and then at the end of the story proclaim the good news in 'the city' was a particularly evocative metaphor for the group to pick up on in relation to 'faithful capital' existent within their communities. For while 'deserts, mountains and seas are all places in which the behaviours contrary to the civilized behaviour of the cities occurs' (Stewart 2007:216), the participants saw that Devonport more readily aligned itself with these 'uncivilized' places of chaos rather than the city within the narrative. The fact that the Church had remained in the community, to perform baptisms and funerals and provide some community endeavours, including 'friendly wives' who host outings, art, craft and cookery events, was seen as a positive characteristic. There was yet hope to transform their city into a 'home' and provide, through faithful capital, a 'homecoming' welcome.

Displacement, the theme of the final biblical narrative (Luke 9.46–52), also struck a ready chord with the group. Devonport was cast as a fundamentally migrant place (with a large influx of asylum-seekers). They also noticed how the physical and social environment of their area had changed in the last 20 years, but put great stock in the rebirth of the place in the regeneration plan. The Christian 'sojourner' motif was a powerful one within a context where migrancy was a constant reminder that the whole inhabited earth, not just a particular building, was the space of divine presence. It is no coincidence, as Timothy Gorringe reminds us, that when Paul speaks about mission and the 'building' of a community, as well as encouraging a people (1 Cor. 10.23; 1 Thess. 5.11), 'the metaphorical use of the word points to a profound truth about the built environment. Form follows function; buildings serve a purpose [they] make moral statements' (Gorringe 2002:1).

The ageing and regeneration (or 'building up') of landscapes was also commented upon in relation to the graveyard of the church, which now serves as a community park (converted in the 1960s with headstones being relocated to the perimeter and older headstones forming a central walkway through the park). Many stories were connected with this place, including the rather gruesome eighteenth-century murder of a dockyard clerk in the graveyard, the trial of the two perpetrators, and the seven-year public display of their decomposing bodies in iron cages! Doris Francis *et al.*, in their analysis of contemporary cemetery practice, note the significance of the reinterpretation of older burial grounds into urban green space or heritage sites. They link the cemetery as garden to the emblematic power of the Garden of Eden, focused on a beautiful landscape and notions of home where relationships among distant kin 'are made material' (Francis *et al.* 2005:198). Such reascription of cemeteries also has an important part to play in 'place-making' endeavours, for they are sites that heighten personal consciousness and act as powerful 'repositories of group identity and collective memory'. Commemoration involves a literal 'calling to mind' of a particular narrative. Such events, stories and places 'underscore the communal responsibilities of the present generation as the custodians of the group's heritage to maintain and protect the other' (Francis *et al.* 2005:201). Jonathan Z. Smith (1987) similarly contends that ritual brings places into being – sacralization produces meaningfulness. The community thus realized that the park area of the graveyard in fact fostered rituals of 'sitting peacefully', 'eating picnics', 'children playing', which all in some small way formed a part of the contemporary 'rituals' of homemaking.

Devonport: building a New Jerusalem?

The Faith and Quality of Life Strategy, as part of the regeneration plan within Devonport, is an important step towards the 'up-building' of the place (in both physical and social terms). In the Contextual Bible Studies one of the most interesting images of Devonport that emerged was the participants' 'organic' conception of it as a place that had deep wounds but was also, through the regeneration project, starting to experience healing. The personality and character of the city was brought to the fore most arrestingly in the conception of it as the 'faraway' country and place of dissolute living in the parable of the lost son and in its historical reputation as a 'rebellious place', where cannons faced inwards to the people but where also 'powers from below' could unsettle and effect change. Adam Reed, in his ethnographic study of interpretations of the personality of London, offers interesting reflections on how not only can people animate a city but also how a city in turn plays a part in animating

Figure 4.2 Reinterpreting graves: Stoke Damerel church park

or characterizing them (2002). It seems the personality ascribed to Plymouth had a part to play in the galvanization of the community to work for social transformation. The city was a memory world that could activate 'the biographical and ancestral memory of its subjects' (Reed 2002:135). The radical personification could offer potent resistance to damaging 'dominant' narratives. Reed also notes how anthropological readings of cities should attend to description by inhabitants rather than just looking at social or economic processes to get a 'sense of the place' and what needs doing to make it more 'homely' (Reed 2002:129). All participants in the contextual reading submitted that the 'place-making' welcome of warmth and relationship was a central image for them to build upon in conceiving of the word in their largely migrant place. The cemetery as park became a particularly potent symbol of the reappropriation of place and rituals for community building.

Gorringe reminds us that the antidote to 'structural sins' in cities are forms and expressions of grace: those elements that 'give pleasure, raise the spirit or proclaim the world home in suburban gardens, in city streets and parks, in the alleys and narrow lanes of villages'

(Gorringe 2002:221). The faithful capital residing in Devonport and the honesty with which people contextualized and were challenged by the biblical stories is surely an important part of the story of re-birth in that place.

5

Reading in a rural village

Beware then of the idyll implicit in the well-kept fields and the neat hedgerows ... for the idyll of the countryside is riddled with uncertainty.

Tom Ang

Artists, writers, poets and playwrights have variously inscribed the romantic picture of a 'rural idyll'. That is, the myth of the calming constancy and tranquillity of rural life and its welcome respite from the chaotic urban realm. The distinction between the rural and urban spheres has been a traditional theme of Western thought, summed up in William Cowper's dictum that 'God made the country, and man made the town' (cited in Gorringe 2002:117). Even in ancient times rural and city life were often pitted against one another in moralizing tracts. The city was pictured as a domain of vice and competition and the country, in contrast, as a domain of virtue and concord. Moreover, the latter provided an escape from the perils of the former. Horace writes:

> Happy is the man who remains far from the world of business ... who avoids the forum and the haughty thresholds of our more important citizens. Instead he trains the mature tendrils of his grapevines ... stands in a secluded valley and surveys his herds of lowing cattle as they graze ... how pleasant it is to lie down sometimes under an ancient oak ... meanwhile the stream glides by between its high banks and the birds warble in the trees. (Horace, *Epodes* 2:1–26)

Likewise for Cicero, 'nothing could be happier than a farmer's life, not only because of the public service he performs, since agriculture is advantageous to the whole human race, but also because of pleasure' (Cicero, 'An Essay on Old Age', 16:55–6).

In some biblical traditions, farming likewise provides the context for certain hopes to be fulfilled. The land on which one labours becomes part and parcel not only of the cultural heritage of one's immediate kin but also the very identity of Israel, the people of God, whose inhabitation of the land depends on covenantal fidelity. In the parables of Jesus the countryside often features as a place of fecundity, sustenance and return. Ploughing and harvesting, two central agricultural pursuits, become suggestive emblems for the planting of the Kingdom (Luke 9.62) and the imminent judgement that Jesus announces (Matt. 9.37–38; Luke 10.2). Rural land is also seen as a place of relief and restoration that Jesus frequently retreats to from busy urban centres (Matt. 14.23; Luke 6.12).

If rural areas are venerated in selected biblical writings, sociocultural studies of the first century have to a certain extent exploded the myth of an ancient Mediterranean rural idyll. Under Roman imperial rule a minority (often urban) elite consumed the majority of profits: high taxation, rents and tolls. Extractive policies and land confiscation led to poverty, debt, social unrest and banditry among the non-elite rural dwellers. These 'bandits' were political protesters, 'their targets were primarily the urban elites and the large estate holders' (Hanson and Oakman 1998:90). Ekkehard and Wolfgang Stegemann paint a similarly dismal picture of rural life:

> The vast majority of the rural populace in antiquity lived on the fine line between hunger and assurance of subsistence. The reasons for this are to be found in fields that on average, were much too small, the catastrophic consequences of crop failures, and above all in over-taxation and overindebtedness of small farmers. Especially the simple rural people – that is, the great majority of the population as a whole – apparently lived with constant concern about achieving the means of survival.   (Stegemann and Stegemann 1999:51)

In contemporary contexts similarly, costly developments, including government agricultural policy, poor farm earnings, low-wage economy, unfair trade patterns and, most arrestingly, the 2001 outbreak of foot and mouth disease – described by some as the 'most serious economic and social crisis experienced by rural communities' in recent years (Rodway-Dyer and Shaw 2005:63) – have served to remind us all of the fragility and vulnerability inherent in rural life. The stark images of burning carcasses of slain cattle displayed in the media graphically disturbed the serene and pleasant landscapes more normally brought to mind by the rural idyll vision. However, despite the hardships faced by the traditional rural industries, for some at least, the 'rural idyll' myth is still persuasive. The continued migration of middle-class urban dwellers to rural areas seems symptomatic of the enduring appeal of this romantic idea. Problems associated with the rural economy can often be neatly shelved under 'food and farming' concerns (Martineau 2004:4) not directly relevant to the lives of the urban to rural 'exile'.

John Saxbee, in his essay 'A Country Retreat' (2004), categorizes ways in which an urban–rural interchange in the pursuit of spiritual advance and refreshment has been constructed. First, the countryside attracts commuters, those who want to inhabit a pleasant environment when they are *not* at work (2004:7). Second are those who retire to the countryside in search of a 'place to live before they die' (2004:7). Third are those who buy second homes as 'country retreats'. Fourth are those who holiday in rural areas, and fifth are day-trippers for whom walking and fresh air associated with rural areas is highly valued (2004:8–9). Saxbee celebrates the ritual retreat of these (former) urban dwellers and provides a theological rationale for such moves by noting that the 'Aramaic basis of the name Jesus means, "to bring into open space"' (2004:9). However, Saxbee is also not blind to the threats of 'displacement' within such urban-to-rural relocations: 'Exodus from the anonymity of the city is accompanied by a sense of being exiled from the privileges of privacy, not least in matters to do with personal faith and morality' (Saxbee 2004:12). One could also add that for many of the groups identified, true relationships with the rural context are not always propagated. The commuter turns the rural environment into a 'dormitory' space; the retired keep firm kinship links with the place from which they moved, perhaps to the neglect of their immediate contexts; the second-home buyers effectively promote empty spaces within rural areas, devoid of human interaction for extended periods of time. It seems ironic, then, that implicit within the mentality of those buying into the rural idyll myth are the seeds of that myth's very destruction: the picture of 'place' (land, creation, people, tradition and story in harmony) is deconstructed through these dynamics into Augé's 'non-place'. 'For the newcomers, the village is not necessarily the focus of their social life and even their leisure may often take place outside the village' (Hunt and Satterlee 1986:522). It was with these mixed insights that I approached a rural village in Dartmoor National Park, Drewsteignton.

Contextual readings from Drewsteignton

Drewsteignton is in many ways the quintessential Devon village and epitome of the 'rural idyll' image. The square, complete with church, two pubs and a post office, exudes charm in a picture post-card sort of way. The parish boundaries are, as one guidebook cover states, 'spread wide, cascading over the rolling hills of the Dartmoor borderlands where small farmsteads nestle in wooded combes' (Curno 2001). The Teign valley cuts through the land nearby and the grand ramparts of Castle Drogo, the youngest castle in Britain, survey the village from above.

Several of the inhabitants, both old (who have lived all their life there) and new (many young professionals or retirees who have chosen to escape the treadmill of urban life to settle into a quieter rural setting), within the village are, in principle, keen to foster place awareness. Community, on the surface, is for the most part strong: book groups, gardening clubs, artistic clusters and the church all have important cultural parts to play in community life. The volunteer par-ticipants for the Contextual Bible Study ranged in age from thirties to eighties. Though it was not exclusively a 'church' group, church attendees constituted the majority. We met in the village pub, a central focus of the village's life. Interestingly given that the evening was advertised as 'Our Place, Our Hope', it was only (bar one) the relative newcomers to the village that came along (a mere 15 years being the record residence length among attendees). One wonders, along with Saxbee, whether Grace Davie's take on religion in Britain as involving 'believing without belonging' (1994) is actually reversed in the movement of urban to rural dwelling. For some rural incom-ers, what they may or may not believe seems 'secondary to their need to belong' (Saxbee 2004:13). It was perhaps those who had not lived all their lives in the village who most wanted to exhibit and claim a stake in 'Our Place, Our Hope'.

We began, in the spirit of sharing stories, with people revealing facts about themselves and their relationship with Drewsteignton that others in the group would not necessarily know. Many spoke about their lives before moving to the village (some had lived abroad, others had worked in inner cities) and their reasons for moving, in-cluding the heavenly views, a tranquil place to retire and to be nearer family. Others shared even more intimate details, the front room of their cottage that had served as their birthing room, another about a childhood memory of visiting Drewsteignton long ago for a tea party while on holiday. Using the 'ABC sense of place activity', whereby communities are encouraged to think less in a historical or linear sense about their place and more about local distinctiveness (archaeology, architecture, landscape, food, folklore etc.), through an alphabetical pattern that 'shuffles and juxtaposes in ways that surprise' (Clifford and King 2006:xi), we spelled out the letters of DREWSTEIGNTON and encouraged reflections from the group. Many of the elements discussed were celebrating the natural world and non-human creation, and corroborated a picture of rural peace and tranquillity: ducks, dogs, rabbits, eggs, water, wildlife, trees, elderflowers, early morning sunrises, gardens, gorse, grass, trees, the River Teign, orchids, night skies and new lambs. The sense of rural respite was also conveyed with people naming recreation, solace, environment, inspiration and neighbourliness as central dynamics of life in Drewsteignton. The positive view of the built environment was summed up in images of resources (pubs, shop, church), thatched roofs, narrow lanes and protection by the National Trust. People were also mentioned within the exercise: wee ones, teenagers and pensioners, themselves testimony to the life-stages lived there. In nearly every instance in the activity, the concepts forwarded by the group were entirely positive, with only two notable exceptions which belied deeper fractures in the seemingly peaceful idyll image: 'dos and don'ts' (implying some power plays over accepted practices or land uses in the area) and 'overpriced housing', which was identified as having a direct effect on the village's demography: younger people could not afford to live in the village.

Luke 15, the parables of the lost sheep, coin and son, stimulated the group to discuss four 'place' issues: first, about various manifestations of 'loss' within their personal lives and community; second, the logic of leaving the 'collective' in order to retrieve the 'individual'; third, the possible resonance of the shepherd, woman, sinner, coin and son within their context; fourth, the parables' invitation to action in their twenty-first-century situation. On the theme of loss in personal lives and the community, various elements of community life that had been lost over the years were lamented. The loss of the school, quarry and butcher's shop (along with the livelihoods they all sustained) had been a blow to the village, as had the loss of a resident rector, living in the village. Interestingly, the one 'place'

Figure 5.1 The village shop and post office, Drewsteignton

within the village that all agreed they would willingly give up everything to retain was not the church building, but rather the shop. This
stood as the living heart of the community: all residents used and
depended on its service, something that could not be said for any other
physical site.

Next, the logic (or lack of it) of the shepherd leaving his 99 sheep
in the wilderness, a place that represented harshness and danger, was
considered. Many agreed that it would surely have been better for
him to cut his losses and stick with the greater number. One participant who trains teachers mentioned that the golden rule of
childcare is never to leave the majority in order to seek out the
single wanderer. Others realized, however, that often parables make
points through subversive avenues; they are not plain stories which
can be easily understood or allegorized. On the contrary, they assault
the senses into alternative ways of thinking. At the root of both illustrations was the maxim that in order to gain something of worth,
you have to let go of something dear to you. In relation to the church
community, this perhaps meant rethinking how it traditionally
operated and worshipped in order to have greater appeal to those

outside. On a deeper level, and a theme that would be developed further in conversation within the group, was whether the 'ideal' picture of the rural idyll needed to be let go or 'muddied' in the imaginations of some inhabitants in order to be more inclusive of those people and practices that don't easily fit the image.

In considering the possible resonance of the shepherd, woman, sinner and coin within Drewsteignton, very interesting was the fact that the majority of the group immediately identified themselves and the church community with the shepherd and woman rather than the 99 sheep, let alone the lost sheep or coin. While the loss of 'bums on seats' in church was bemoaned, only one participant shrewdly noted that the 'majority' actually existed outside the church, and that the church should be very careful about immediately casting folks outside its walls as the 'sinner' (lost sheep and coin) role. One participant quoted a recent survey of the nation's best-loved books that ranked *Pride and Prejudice* at the top and put the Bible at number four, much higher than our national literary treasure, Shakespeare. The participant noted that this ranking was surely surprising given that we live in a so-called 'post-Christian' age. He also wagered that this would seem to indicate that those people in the village who do not attend the church are not 'lost' or anti-faith, but rather themselves symptomatic of a wider trend in contemporary Britain of 'believing without belonging'.

In thinking about the invitation to action given by the parables, the group agreed that the collective community should have a crucial part to play in creating a healthier, more united society. Increasingly 'individualism' and free choice is prized over collective models of community that are ever more threatened. Indeed, seen in this light, the parable of the lost sheep could very well be seen as an invitation to seek out and challenge 'individualistic' modes and encourage the rehabilitation of a collective ethos of community. Luke's parable of the lost son was a story evocative enough to provoke a human reaction, with or without a faith background. Predictably enough the first reaction voiced was about the unjust treatment of the elder brother, with whom most of the sympathies of the group lay. Very interesting was one participant's input, who himself was born a farmer's elder son and therefore could readily empathize with the character's predicament. In farming families in Devon, the elder son often gets paid precious little, lives in rented accommodation, and to all intents and purposes has to wait his turn to step into his dead father's shoes. The participant reflected on how in some families the father would not give up the reins in his lifetime and resentment and animosity grew within the unit as a result. He also spoke of a certain jealousy of the younger son's freedom to pursue his own dreams, even if in the end, within the story, they lead him into misery.

Others spoke about known family feuds over inheritances and someone else imagined a smallholding father in Drewsteignton dividing his inheritance within his lifetime: he would have to remortgage half his land to produce the capital to give to the younger son and as a result would have plunged himself and the elder son into relative poverty, given that farmers faced pinches on all sides, only exacerbated by certain government policies and recent catastrophic outbreaks of disease (BSE, foot and mouth). This has some resonance with those studies that reveal that young farmers increasingly have to borrow their father's equipment and go out and earn their own money, as the father cannot afford to pay them wages comparable with young men who work in the urban centres (Scott cited in Curno 2001:14).

This conveniently, in place terms, brought the conversation to the theme of home and relationships. Given that most participants were 'incomers' to the village this raised some remarkable reflections. Many spoke about their feeling of rootedness within Drewsteignton despite only being there a relatively short time. Many admitted to often verbally referring to 'home' as the place where one was born and grew up, or where one's family resided, but still all agreed that present roots were cultivated and tended in the village. Sheldrake's definition of home as a place where we reside through certain stages of our life, a place where we feel part of a community, a place that promotes a relationship with the natural landscape and a place that offers access to the sacred, seemed to resonate with one young couple's reflections on their search for an alternative way of life in the village.

The movement of incomers on the demographics and fortunes of the village was acknowledged as a double-edged sword, especially for those who had lived in the village over a decade and brought up their children there. In the 1970s there were fewer people living in the village than there had been in the times of the Domesday records. It was in fact a dying village, but the collapse of the housing market in the early 1990s finally provided a small window of opportunity for younger families to buy properties within the area. One participant even told, with wry humour, the story of the local incumbent who could hardly remember conducting a wedding service, given that he had spent so many years burying his parishioners. Given the large influx of middle-class dwellers, others bemoaned the fact that, unlike the lost son, many of the children of the village who had gone away to study were not able, because of the rise in house prices, to now 'come home'. (West Devon has one of the largest national discrepancies between average income at £15,500 and the price of the average starter home at £129,000.) As employment was largely found in low-paid tourism, service or land-labour industries this far exceeded their means. Others revealed that while Drewsteignton was not dominated by, it certainly was not immune to, a commuter and second-home culture. (It was estimated that 17 dwellings were holiday cottages.) One participant, who worked at the pub, bemoaned the fact that many professionals who commuted did not spend their money or time supporting local businesses. The fact that we physically conducted the Bible study within the pub brought reflection on this particular place: for some locals the pub constituted the centre of social life. However, for other incomers the quaint thatched roof perhaps struck a redolent chord of a 'perfect village pub' full of 'merry rustics who would recount tales of traditional village life'. It was perhaps no coincidence that I could not persuade a group of 'indigenous' ale drinkers to participate in the Contextual Bible Study. Could it be that they found my intrusion, like the intrusion of many incomers, a cause of resentment, while in contrast 'the newcomers may find the locals hostile and unfriendly; hence the village pub may itself become a reason for conflict' (Hunt and Satterlee 1986:523).

The group went on to reflect on Augé's theme of non-place as a result of technological advances. Many felt that increasingly global lines of communication diminished the energy available for face-to-face interaction with the people in one's place. Anna Markusen, in her article 'The Work of Forgetting and Remembering Places', likewise submits that 'the availability of these alternative networks and communities real and created erodes the bonds of local companionship and dilutes people's sense of responsibility to others in their local communities' (2004:2313). In many ways the ability to conduct life from a computer had similar consequences to those who conducted their lives in an urban centre nearby but still hankered for a stake in a solid and peaceful vision of rural life, if only to sleep there! Related to this, often the so-called 'drawbridge effect' is operative; this is when incomers and second-home owners don't want the village to change in any way from the 'rural idyll' they feel they have bought into, but they often don't fully participate in those traditions. In this respect, the people who reside there threaten the place itself with 'displacement'. In Bernard Deacon's words:

> The new regional community is in some respects therefore a community out of space, one located in a particular space but locked into networks that extend well beyond that space. Their [incomers and second-home owners] class (or perhaps gender) background predispose them towards a discourse of leisure or tourism-related to 'quality of life' because that is the aspect of the regional territory they are most likely to have previously encountered. But, in inserting this aspect into the everyday discussion of their community they exclude other sectors and communities for whom quality of life has no meaning.
>
> (2004:221)

Various reflections on the theme of those 'out of place' were prompted by reflection on the story of the boy in the temple (Luke 2.41–52). While the image of the young Jesus teaching the learned teachers of the law was seen as counter-cultural for that time, the group wondered whether the richness of the experience of older people is, in our culture, largely ignored, but is one similarly that can bring the unexpected. In an era that celebrates youth and potential, the fact that older people are rich repositories of history and experience was seen as valuable in the construction and maintenance of a collective sense of place. The mapping activity that supplemented the Bible study asked people to locate areas of conflict within the village; this immediately started to scratch below the surface of the more positive pictures given in the first activity, the ABC of place. One participant noted how the parish boundary had recently been changed to include the nearby villages of Whiddon Down and Crockernwell, but that the attitudes of inhabitants were far harder to remodel. Indeed a parish plan was being constructed to take account of these developments and try to foster solidarity rather than suspicion among the communities. The physical space of the church was marked on the map by all participants, without exception, as a place of conflict. Reasons included a plan to build executive homes and social housing on the land surrounding the church. No rector residing in the vicarage was seen as the loss of an 'open space' for hospitality and welcome to the whole village; the use of the interior space of the church for social activities, children's meals and the movement of pews also caused unrest. Outside the church, people identified the proposal for a traveller encampment by the village as a source of conflict. Such oppositions are common in environments like Drewsteignton, for travellers are seen to 'dis-order' the maintenance of the rural idyll image. In Gorringe's words, 'What replaces the gamekeepers and the mantraps is political nimbyism, the determination to keep middle-class quality of life at all costs, and a savage attack on those who threaten to spoil it, from New Age travellers to gypsies' (Gorringe 2002:127).

The largely mono-cultural perceptions that dominated the village were also identified as a source of potential exclusion. One school teacher who had worked in a multicultural city before moving to the area, voiced concern about the very strong ideological maps of 'insider' and 'outsider' that the village children sometimes seemed to operate by; the negative suspicions surrounding urban life infiltrating the village also had a part to play here. In essence the very white, middle-class projection of the village's demographic could link it to what David Sibley has called 'geographies of exclusion'. Race, age and colour can discursively, even if not intentionally, produce 'outsiders' in the imaginations of the inhabitants. Abstraction, Sibley says, is the urge to 'make separations between ordered and disordered, us and them'; if these take hold, however, separation occurs. This is 'a process of purification' and 'the means by which defilement or pollution is avoided' (Sibley 1995:37).

This particular 'exclusionary' trait came much more to the fore in the reading of the stilling of the storm and the exorcism of Legion (Luke 8.22–39). The contextualizing of evil, chaos and the demonic within Drewsteignton was harder than for the inner-city group. The chaos of the storm was seen as a quasi-personal evil that threatened to drown 'other' people, but not the community. The group also did not picture Legion as a multiple, fragmented locality. Much of the group's conversations revolved around the fact that Legion could be suffering from schizophrenia, psychoses or personality disorders.

Some mentioned Hogarth's arresting pictures of life in a madhouse to visualize such physical and mental ailments. The group focused on the fact that Jesus rejects Legion's request to live with him and instead sends him back to his home territory. I was left wondering to some extent whether Legion, as an outsider, could have a place. All in all there seemed to be a strong awareness of the limits of the community as portrayed in the story and a certain limit on the depth of healing that could occur for the mentally tortured Legion. While, after the session, participants noted that alcoholism has 'possessed' various individuals within Drewsteignton this was not mentioned within the group in the Contextual Bible Study. There seemed an initial reticence to talk about Legion occupying the rural idyll. Paul Cloke *et al.* have revealed that 'socioculturally rural residents often deny that problems exist in the areas they inhabit. Here the pervasive myth of the rural idyll seems to be strong still' (Cloke *et al.* 2002, cited in Cresswell 2004:114). Those that do not fit the 'pure space' ideal envisaged by both populace and policy-makers are effectively excluded not only spatially but also within the thoughts and worldview of the community. In David Sibley's words:

> A rigid stereotype of place, the English countryside, throws up discrepant others. These groups are other, they are folk-devils, and they transgress only because the countryside I defend is stereotypical pure space that cannot accommodate difference.
>
> (Sibley 1995, quoted in Cloke *et al.* 2000:727)

The last biblical story on the theme of displacement (Luke 9.46–52) once more provided thoughts on the status of children, given the centrality of the child image as representative of the disciple. While the elderly as rich 'chests of community meaning' had been celebrated earlier, now it was seen that if stories became nostalgic there could be a danger of resistance to change within the community. The image of 'following' was also seen as a challenge, for there is always security in the static and known, rather than the changing and unknown. One farmer noted that there are misleading and distorting images of the past, which hanker after outdated heroes and role models. The farmer found the saying 'leave the dead to bury their dead' particularly enlightening in this respect. Calling to mind the pyres of dead cattle in the foot and mouth crises, he offered the rhetorical remark: 'Let the corpses pile up. This story is then not

Figure 5.2 Drewsteignton village square

a question of whether to stay or to go, it is rather a question of attitude and heart: what is the urgent concern?' His frank acceptance of the non-negotiable fact of change within rural life was a stark contrast to many of the others within the group. Perhaps it is not surprising that 'death' should be so readily contextualized by a farmer. Saxbee revealed that death in the countryside is a profound motif; while city inhabitants may be anaesthetized to death, for the rural dweller 'death is a fact of life' (Saxbee 2004:14) and can function as a profound metaphor for social life there. The group's experience of the 'nearness' of the cycle of seasons also meant that the images of lilies in the field and birds of the air were readily contextualized in Drewsteignton, though interestingly the 'artefact centred view of the landscape as an aesthetic object' (Riley and Harvey 2005:272) still dominated for some.

Drewsteignton: some conclusions

I have reported some dominant trends within a reading group consisting of people who are largely incomers to a rural village. Not all shared similar views and many people who resided in Drewsteignton all their lives would probably give a very different ethnographic account. One of the main differences between the contextualizing process in this rural context and the city context outlined in the previous chapter has been the fact that most participants initially gave a very positive view of their place (valuing the environment, fabric and perceived social solidarity of the village). The theme of 'home' became a dominant trope for those families who had opted to live in a rural community. Cloke reveals, however, that often this ideal of 'domestic life' can also mask deep fissures in the reality of rural life: 'Being with a home, then, in geographical space where the imagined geography is one where the home is valorised to this extent, is once again to transgress the sociocultural meanings and moralities which lie at the heart of rural life' (Cloke *et al.* 2002, cited in Cresswell 2004:114). The influx of middle classes to rural areas can drive social problems to ground. For the incomer or second-home owner, the 'rural idyll' can be but a 'village in the mind', the mythical place 'beyond the high-rise flats and the Chinese take-aways' (Newby 1977, cited in Hunt and Satterlee 1986:521), not a village of reality. Without honest confrontations with the 'hidden transcript' (the voices that tell a different story from the dominant, elite vision) of rural life, the 'idyll' becomes a dangerous and exclusive 'idol'.

The romantic vision was, of course, questioned and challenged by the reactions of the group to the themes of those 'out of place' and 'sustainability'. The very real and honest acknowledgement of conflict and economic hardship (including high house prices) also served as an important levelling mechanism to balance the initial largely positive pictures of life conveyed in Drewsteignton by the participants. It was also realized that if such cracks are not acknowledged one is able to perpetuate a vision of 'undisturbed' rural life, which necessarily 'excludes' certain groups (in this case alcoholics, travellers etc.). The group compared the cyclical changes in the seasons implicit in the biblical images of nature with the recent challenges encountered by farmers in the area. Such experiences offered wisdom about the necessity of change and the importance of a willingness to transform and be 'permeable to new people and ideas' (Clifford and King 2006:xi).

6

Reading in a fishing village

Fishing is not merely a job, it is a way of life.

Rob van Ginkel

The county of Cornwall sits at the south-western tip of Great Britain. Like many peninsulas, surrounded by seas to the north, south and west, it has often been conceptualized as a 'border place' (Mackey 2002:16). Boundaries in spatial terms do not only mark ends but also beginnings; it is from boundaries that new horizons can be encountered. This feature undoubtedly contributes to the relationships forged between people and environment in the county. Sally Mackey, in her study of landscape and memory in Cornwall, cites informants who recall childhood memories, collective memories and site-specific memories in their defining of place and identity in the region: 'everything went by boat; everything went out that way'; 'the sea, the moon, and the edge of the cliffs and the issues threatening where we live obviously influence us' (Mackey 2002:16).

Anthropologists have likewise long recognized how memory and story connect people and landscapes in intricate webs of significance. Often such narratives and recollections do not offer objective fact but something far more interesting to the ethnographer: evidence of how people construct their particular sense of place and identity in relation to their physical land. Simon Schama, in his celebrated cross-cultural work, *Landscape and Memory* (1995), connected the importance of landscapes, both material and mythological, in the construction of identity. He writes: 'Before it can ever be repose for the senses, landscape is the work of the mind. Its scenery is built up as much from strata of memory as from layers of rock' (1995:6–7). To give just a couple of examples, the coastal Yolunu people in Blue Mud Bay, North Australia use 'sea' and 'water' (and their ebb and flow) to symbolically construct ancestry, kinship and marriage (Morphy and Morphy 2006:62). The Yolunu are by no means unique in identifying themselves and their relationships with images of sea and water. As Veronica Strang points out, until recently water 'was the major "mirror" for many people . . . it is therefore not surprising to find recurrent cosmological ideas in which water is believed to hold the image or spirit of the person' (2004:92). In a related vein, the Native American Apache peoples see land as central to human ontology. Keith Basso attests, 'Such locations, charged as they are with personal and social significance work in important ways to shape the images that Apache have – or should have – of themselves' (Basso 1996, cited in Bird 2002:523). When narratives are forgotten in common consciousness, the Apache depict their demise as a literal 'loss of the land' (see Bird 2002:523).

While 'social' location (i.e. sex, race, class, religion, politics) is central to Fernando Segovia and Mary Ann Tolbert's edited collection *Reading from this Place* (1995), it is also important to remember that geography and topography have important parts to contribute to 'context'. Topography is literally 'of, or relating to, the physical features of the earth' (Malbon 1986:51). Embodiment in, and reflection on, how a physical landscape shapes you is a central part of any interpretative endeavour. The Bible also reflects a world-view in which landscapes in general and 'seas and waters' in particular become evocative 'characters' within its narratives. The sea is at once a source of food, livelihood and, through its parting in the Exodus tradition, liberation. Baptismal theology likewise denotes water as a material symbolic of cleansing and rebirth in Christ. But seas and waters are not universally conceived positively in biblical texts, they also evoke the dangerous, demonic and deadly. Images of sea and storm are used symbolically within the biblical tradition and often represent the primeval sea of watery chaos. It is no coincidence that the beast in Revelation emerges from a frenzied seascape (Rev. 13.1). The sea is also used to present figuratively the tumult of the people (Ps. 65.7), the 'roaring' of attacking militia (Jer. 6.23), and a force of malevolence (though God has ultimate power to divide, still and conquer it (Job 38.8–11; Ps. 29)). Dreaded floods reap chaos on creation, destroying 'all flesh in which is the breath of life' (Gen. 6.17); a squall on Lake Galilee threatens to submerge and drown the fisher people and their livelihoods there (Matt. 8.23–27; Luke 8.22–25).

The 'industry of the sea', fishing, also becomes symbolic of judgement in the New Testament. Disciples are charged with the task of 'fishing for people' (Matt. 4.19) and accordingly the Kingdom is imaged as a dragnet that gathers multiple fish, which will be sorted into respective baskets of good and evil 'at the end of the age'. Moreover, as Michael Northcott reminds us, in the parable of the dragnet it is the fish caught on the hook or in the net of the fishermen that are visual metaphors of salvation, not living fish in the water (2008:242–3). The early Christians even adopted the symbol of the fish to represent their movement, *ichthus* being a convenient acronym of the Greek 'Jesus Christ, Son of God, Saviour'. Such symbolic import is perhaps not surprising given the fact that fishing environments constituted major backdrops for the Galilean Jesus movement, and fish was a staple part of the diet of the region. The centrality of the fishing industry is inscribed in place names in the area: Bethsaida literally translates as 'fishing village', and Tarichaeae, the Greek name for Magdala, has been (tongue in cheek) translated as 'processed fishville' (Hanson and Oakman 1998:110). Not that the fishing industry and the metaphors it birthed should be romanticized in any way, quite the opposite, the Palestinian fisherman's lot was not an easy one. Cicero famously declared that in the rank of occupations in the ancient world the fisherman was the lowest (Cicero cited in Carter 2000:121). Similarly Hanson and Oakman reveal that even fishermen who owned their boats in the period were still subject to very strict regulations, for 'fishing was controlled by the ruling elites. The local rulers sold fishing rights to brokers who in turn contracted with fishers' (1998:106). The Galilean fishing economy thus included fishing families who were 'the primary labourers who caught the fish' and 'formed cooperatives in order to bid for fishing contracts or leases'. Hired labourers were also used to help with 'manning oars, mending and washing nets'. Fish processors prepared harvests for markets, but their work was also heavily taxed (Hanson and Oakman 1998:107). Fish were claimed as part of the revenue of the empire and fisher-folk paid taxes both on their yields and transportation (see Carter 2000:121).

If it is true that 'places are brought into being in the mind as much as they are on land' (Paulsen 2004:244), then images that aid imagination and inspire both change and critique are themselves crucial parts of the stimulation of place. Henri Lefebvre spoke of 'the imagination of place' within societies as a tool for rehabilitation or change, particularly as a 'creative impulse from the underside of society' and a 'subversive form of power' (Lefebvre 1991, discussed in Moxnes 2003:148). It is in this vein that Jesus offers a forceful comment on hierarchical imperial impositions on the fishing industry and posits an alternative economy based on fictive kinship and other-regard when he charters them to fish for people. In his miraculous feedings by multiplication of fish 'Jesus enacts an alternative to the imperial market economy by sharing and multiplying resources' (Carter 2000:328). The Eucharist itself, which may have been framed, as Northcott has argued, by a fish meal, was 'a miracle of sharing': 'in the setting of the impoverishing extractive economy of Roman Imperial occupation an act of blessing, breaking and sharing on this scale was a meal which turned itself into an act of resistance to empire' (Northcott 2008:237). It is no accident that among those fishing villagers living an economically perilous subsistence under Roman jurisdiction should be the people among whom 'God's empire is first manifested' (Carter 2000:121) and from whom key symbolic images for the early Christian movement were drawn.

James Acheson notes in his cross-cultural study of contemporary fishing practice that the industry is still precarious and vulnerable with prices fluctuating daily in fish markets and good sea harvests not necessarily guaranteeing healthy income for those who risk their lives to bring the fish home. Fishermen often receive pay according to a portion of the catch, rather than 'a flat fee or wage' (Acheson 1981:278). Further pressures have come with recent government directives regarding fish quotas and sea ownership.

With these concerns in mind, contemporary communities dependent on fishing are perhaps uniquely placed to contextualize and re-imagine aspects of their own place and experience in reference to biblical stories. These connections feature, as will be seen, in the following record of a Contextual Bible Study in the Cornish fishing village of Newlyn.

Contextual readings from Newlyn

Newlyn has fewer than 5000 inhabitants. It is one of the most active operational fishing ports in Britain, landing fish to the value of around 18 million pounds sterling per annum. Unlike many other areas in Cornwall, Newlyn does not enjoy large tourist interest (it has only two hotels) and, as a result, has avoided many of the contests

Figure 6.1 Newlyn harbour

surrounding the representation of place to visitors that has dogged other areas in the county (anglicization, dissonant heritages etc.; see Hale 2001:185–96). However, the reopening of the art gallery and the legacy of the famous nineteenth-century 'Newlyn School' (a group of artists who resided in the village in the late nineteenth and early twentieth centuries and specialized in painting that emphasized natural light and often depicted local fishing scenes) has attracted more sightseers to the area each year. Despite its truly beautiful natural environment, Newlyn, in common with many other areas in Cornwall, contains pockets of abject (often hidden) social poverty. Seasonal and minimal-wage employment, along with short-term contracts, has marred the village economy. Indeed economic de-generation in the traditional industries of mining and fishing in the county has left Cornwall statistically among the most deprived counties in Britain (Williams 2003:55).

Newlyn today retains something of its traditional appeal. It has a low percentage of second homes (11 per cent) in comparison to other villages nearby and is strongly connected to the fishing indus-try, which has been the source of the village's income and identity.

T. H. Andrew, in an article published in *Man* in 1921, offers us a portrait of the so-called 'Cornish Fishing Type' in part based on his fieldwork in Newlyn:

> The men are of medium height and occasionally above it, sturdy and stoutly built, with big bones, strong necks and rather round heads. The young men and women attain early maturity, and are often very handsome . . . They take to the sea like a duck takes to water, and are rarely found from it. They make seamen of exceptional skill and daring. The western fishing fleet are largely manned by them, many of them join the Royal Navy as boys and the coxswain of any west-country lifeboat is pretty sure to be one of them.
>
> (Andrew 1921:138)

Today in Newlyn swarthy, handsome types were still to be seen on the harbourside, though I met with a rather more mixed group of people from different occupational and social backgrounds: some had lived in the area all their lives, others were relative newcomers.

An art and crafts group, church community group and a youth dance group variously met for the Contextual Bible Studies in Trinity Methodist Chapel. This building has recently been converted into a community centre offering a wide variety of cultural and leisure pursuits. It has been purposefully designed with the intention to tell stories of the place to its inhabitants (rather than to tourists), in effect to construct an 'authentic place' for the people who live there. Geographers reflecting on the exported 'heritage' image of Cornwall would, I think, be in agreement that the plans for Trinity's conversion 'build in reflexivity and have the ability to promote a range of Cornish historical experiences', and as such be desirable for visitors and cultural activists alike (Hale 2001:194). The fishing industry, art and copper heritage are represented in architectural features of the building: a porch made from the bow of a ship; a font made in the shape of a seashell from local copper; portholes and ropes carefully crafted into the fabric of the building. Indeed the vision of the conversion of the chapel and the linking of story and place seems to hail this initiative as a good example of 'place-making', a place breathing shalom.

We began by focusing on the image of home and journeying in the narrative of the lost son (Luke 15.11–32). Many commented on the low self-esteem of many within the village. Indeed, often those young people perceived as energetic or intellectual left the village to find their fortunes in far-off lands. There was some comfort to be had therefore in the constancy of a 'home' image encountered within the story; lands far beyond Newlyn did not always bring promise and one could return and receive an unquestioning welcome. Those members of the group who remained in the village, however, had their own story to tell about a journey they had embarked upon, which also involved a rapturous homecoming, namely, the adventure involved in the construction of Trinity Methodist Chapel as a multi-purpose community space. The worshipping community left the chapel for a number of years and met in the Seamen's Mission, before returning not to a chapel per se, but a community and arts centre that can be used for worship. Many saw that this new multi-purpose building encapsulated the concept of 'sanctuary' or 'home' far better than the former chapel did as the 'exclusive' place of the church community. Now the young, the elderly and the homeless, as well as performers, artists and creative thinkers, all had a stake in the activities within the centre and by extension their place. The extravagant and inclusive homecoming welcome of the father within the story could be paralleled with this experience. Like the youngest son forced to re-evaluate his position in a country far from home, the time spent in the 'liminal' place of the Seamen's Mission was important in the re-evaluation of home and the re-imagination of place, both physically and socially, within the chapel worshipping community. The Mission to Seafarers has occupied its present building in the village centre since 1911. The huge copper weathervane above the building was made by two craftsmen who were part of a group of artists who sought to provide work for fishermen not needed to go to sea. Thus was born the copper craft industry in the area. The Mission also represents a 'journey' towards the unity of people and place because it bears the first of a series of ten way markers across the village that mark places of interest. Designed by Tom Leaper and sited in 2004, this first symbolic way marker depicts a Bible and cross inside a lifebelt. Villagers felt that not only the copper heritage and its part in the economic sustainability of the community in the early twentieth century, but also the link with the particularity of place, should be echoed within their new building. So a local copper designer was commissioned to incorporate copper crafts within the Trinity Chapel designs. Similarly, participants spoke about the

Figure 6.2 The Centre, Trinity Methodist Chapel

rupture of routine (who sat where; what could or could not be worn/done/said in church) in the Seamen's Mission. This allowed new and less formal patterns of social interaction to be established when they returned (or 'reintegrated' to use Victor Turner's terminology) to life in the chapel building.

In reference to the theme of those 'out of place' and the story of the boy in the temple (Luke 2.41–52), homelessness was identified as a problem for which the 'sanctuary' of the church could be used to offer hospitality (biscuits and a cup of tea) and shelter from the rain. Comments on one particular visitor to the Centre who had voluntarily opted to be homeless (for she did not want to live in a contained shelter) brought some interesting reflections on normalizing 'maps of propriety'. One particularly profound observation in reference to this character was that vulnerable people seemed always to be drawn to extremities and Newlyn geographically as well as socially seemed to strike a chord with this marginal quality. Many participants also noted that the conversion of the church building had galvanized youth and dance group participation and that these young people's potential contribution to the community life (even if

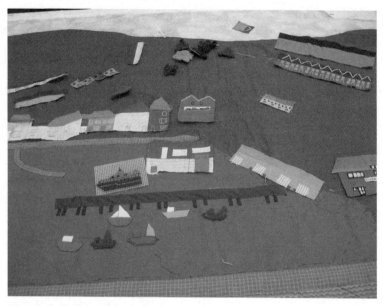

Figure 6.3 Map-making in Newlyn

their 'street' dancing seemed to speak a different cultural language) had been recognized and valued. This underlined that 'out of the mouths of babes' profound lessons could be learnt. The old 'maps of territory' surrounding people's attire and place in church had also been broken in the move to the Seamen's Mission. Stuffiness (imaged in the scholars of the law in the story) had been replaced with freedom (imaged in the child). Now people did not sit in pews, but rather chairs; these were not laid out before services, rather everyone had to pick their own chair up and place it next to another already in the central space. The architecture, likewise, was seen to be more appealing, or less 'alien' to non-religious people; this temple could physically welcome children to teach among the elders. In relation to the mapping activity accompanying the Contextual Bible Study, an arts and craft group set about producing a symbolic 'map' of Newlyn, whereby the Trinity Methodist Chapel was literally and symbolically situated in the 'centre' of the artwork. The sea and coast also took up nearly half of the map, underlining the importance of this as a resource for the village.

The third biblical story, the stilling of the storm and the exorcism of Legion (Luke 8.22–39), perhaps unsurprisingly struck the deepest chord within this fishing environment. The first reaction to the text was, 'Why are professional fishermen asking a carpenter what to do in a crisis?' The group echoed the ancient allegory of the church as a boat traversing the waves of adversity (Günther Bornkamm's redaction-critical reading of Matthew's version of this story is a case in point (1963:57)). The physical space of the chapel also inscribed this allegory. G. Sil, commenting on Christian art on a similar theme, writes:

> The world is a sea in which the Church, like a ship, is beaten by the waves, but not submerged . . . The image lingers in calling the central portion of the church the 'nave' . . . It also appears in the catacombs, as a symbol for the Church, which could survive any disaster.
>
> (Sil 1996:134)

Whether urban congregations miles from the sea would have similarly received Luke's narrative in this way is an open question, but certainly the Newlyn readers readily allegorized their community: even the physical building in which they met was a boat, a vehicle in which to navigate dangerous waters. For Newlyn the fishing trawler, though hazardous, is ultimately the economic life source for the community and in many respects acts as a symbolic identity marker for them. One person, interpreting the boat in the biblical story as the restored chapel building, recounted the story of the *Ripple* (the oldest fishing boat in the British Fishing Vessel Register at 111 years old), which was refurbished and relaunched last year in Newlyn. He noted that like the *Ripple*, with resources and collective will, old institutions (such as the chapel) can and have been restored into new 'seaworthy' vessels of kinship and community. Reflection on the relationship between metaphors such as the 'boat', 'built forms' (such as the Centre) and 'symbolic identity' has been broached by the anthropologist James Fernandez. He maintains that cultural identity is 'negotiated through the interplay of contrasting and/or similar metaphors in language and built environment: metaphors allow one to move from the abstract and inchoate to the concrete and easily graspable' (Fernandez 1974, discussed in Low and Lawrence 1990:472).

Another participant shrewdly commented that Luke does not give any indication of the size or number of crew on the boat and leaves the ownership of the boat open on the narrative level. Historians suggest that in Galilee boats were small and contracted from a boat owner on the understanding that they would be returned safely and unscathed (Keener 1999:278). The discovery in 1986 of a first-century Galilean fishing boat has confirmed that the boat probably had room for four oarsmen, and is estimated to have had around five crew members and a cargo (Hanson and Oakman 1998:110). Though the materials used for building the vessel were very poor – 'inferior wood locally available' – the craftsmanship displayed was great (Crossan and Reed 2001:86). Contextualizing this observation within Newlyn, the participant noted that likewise most trawlers only have a small crew (skipper, mate, engineer and a couple of deck hands). Some boats are owned by a kin group or co-operative, but more usually hired out from a boat owner.

Mounts Bay effectively became the Sea of Galilee within the interpretations of the group. Only this year has Tom Leaper's bronze image of a fisherman throwing a line out to the sea been unveiled. Through the story the group likewise reflected on the true cost to the community of the sea that is both their 'life-giver and taker' (Mackey 2002:15). In Newlyn, one intensely moving account that was shared in response to the sea and windstorm image was the terrible loss of the Penlee lifeboat crew on 19 December 1981. All hands on the lifeboat, *Solomon Browne*, and *The Union Star* (the ship that was being rescued that night) were lost in hurricane conditions. The lifeboat station now stands as a memorial to the bravery of those who voluntarily risked and lost their lives for the sake of others that night. These volunteers did not sleep in a boat when windstorms raged, nor could they halt the elements as the powerful hero in the biblical story did, but bravely stood together to confront the perils before them. The current lifeboat, *Ivan Ellen*, now sits in Newlyn harbour as a visual reminder of all those who make a perilous living from the sea; indeed most of the volunteer crew are themselves fishermen. One participant within the group commented how the stilling of the storm was a hard narrative to digest by families bereaved through perils encountered on the sea. Moreover, picking up on images in the following story of Legion, it is plain to see how painful it is to

Figure 6.4 Penlee lifeboat memorial

imagine the loved ones lost within the 'abyss' – a watery and demonic chaos where the pigs are sent. However, he also recalled how the current crew had stated that when they answer emergency calls, 'We need someone who believes *for* us.' The sleeping stranger in the boat, who exercises divine power and mastery over the unruly elements, and the community meeting in his name, is such an advocate. It has been said on account of events such as this, that in many fishing cultures the sea is interpreted as a boundary marker between life and death. Others have gone so far as to say that Cornish identity is itself built upon lamentations for its lost brothers and sisters: 'departure and death are close cousins here. Both must be mourned in the hope of taming them' (Laviolett 2003:215).

It was Bronislaw Malinowski who first pointed out that ritual and magic tend to be more pervasive in those occupations perceived to be life threatening or dangerous. He noted that in the Trobriand Islands lagoon fishing that held minimal risk and usually could be relied on to offer good yields was not accompanied by ritual or magic. However, the riskier pursuit of open-sea fishing demanded an extensive use of ritual to promote safety and good harvests (Acheson 1981:288). Such coping mechanisms are common in extreme environments, for 'fishermen enter a different realm when they are fishing, and have to be reincorporated into the community when, and if, they return to it, entry and exit between these two spheres is sometimes accompanied by marked rituals' (Acheson 1981:288). The annual Newlyn Fish Festival involves a traditional dedication of the fishing fleets, and offering of prayers for those going out to sea, the vessels to which they entrust their lives and the families they leave behind.

The relationships between the crew members and the 'Master' sleeping soundly also stimulated some interesting discussion among the group. In Newlyn the knowledge of fishing crew relationships actually led to an appealing commentary on the relationships observed in the story. Jesus asks about the crew's faith, which the group in effect interpreted as 'Grow up. I am asleep. You do it!' It is perhaps not surprising that cross-cultural studies of fishing crews have also time and again noted the egalitarian nature of relationships within the boat. This, it is proposed, is in part related to the need for highly skilled hands to face perilous dangers. In such situations the gap between crew and captain necessarily becomes much smaller. Acheson notes:

> . . . from Europe and Latin America to Asia, [a]ll fishing vessels have captains or skippers because of the need to coordinate activities and make definite decisions, but in many crews, the captain's authority is rarely exercised. The ideal skipper–crew relationship is one where crewmen remarked of the skipper 'he's so quiet you hardly know the man is up there' [it's like he is asleep] or 'he hardly says a word, and orders rarely have to be given'.   (Acheson 1981:279)

This co-operative egalitarianism has also translated into various new collective movements within Newlyn to support the entire community. Similar to fishing communities across the world, 'if one cannot control the weather and fish, one can use social ties to organise an effective crew, obtain information on concentrations of fish and have privileged access to them, and be assured of a secure market for the catch' (Acheson 1981:307). One participant mentioned how important the Newlyn Fish Industry Forum was as a tool that empowered not only the crews of boats but also the wider community of the village to take an active charge in their future. The manifesto of the movement claims:

> The forum is an inclusive body, bringing together for the first time all sectors of the industry and including harbour commissioners, community groups, local artists and the public sector. It is therefore a solid private/public partnership united in a common determination to achieve a sustainable regeneration of Newlyn.
>
> (<www.newlyn.org/nifi.htm>)

Others noted how the Cornish disposition was sometimes liable to settle for the status quo and be sceptical that real change could happen. Having a leader (such as the minister who had led the Trinity renovation project) whom they could believe in to effect change within their context was crucial.

The 'journey to the other side' of the lake, as the section immediately following this narrative tells, is a journey towards alien territory (characterized by unclean pigs, tombs, chaos and madness), but it is also ultimately a journey that is paradigmatic of the founding/liberation of a community. Judith Lieu picks up on the postcolonial overtones implicit within the 'exorcism of Legion' narrative following the stilling of the storm; she also conjectures that demonic possession could in fact be symptomatic of a 'society in conflict with itself' (Lieu 1997:66). Whatever the specifics, it is true that Luke wants to show the journey to the other side as a 'stirring up', but also as a saving act that foreshadows Luke's emphasis on universal mission. Lieu writes: 'As a model of the mission of the early church the man is instructed to make known to *his own home* [Gentile] . . . what God has done' (Lieu 1997:66). The association of the 'journey to the other side' with the intent to found a new people was also utilized in responses from individuals in reference to the Trinity project. Former outsiders (people who did not attend the chapel) had been made insiders through participation in the leisure, educational and cultural activities that took place there.

In encountering Legion, the postcolonial locative reading also made sense of the contextualization of perceived 'threats' to the community. Acheson notes that 'the common property nature of marine resources makes fishing a competitive endeavour' (Acheson 1981: 307) and this has informed the conservationist reasoning behind the imposition of government directives regarding quotas. The group revealed that skippers from the village have faced legal proceedings for landing catches in excess of EU fish quotas, proceedings which could result in debilitating financial penalties. Others had protested against the quota measures, which some said were so low a living could barely be made from them; indeed the industry could itself be threatened as a result. There is of course a growing awareness that the sea's resources are not infinite and thus an increasing focus on sustainability and environmental strategies (e.g. new nets reducing the unwanted catch in the trawlers and closed areas for fishing). The group revealed that local fishermen have supported 'rest' times for particular fish fields, a positive step towards the more radical Jubilee principle suggested by The World Summit on Sustainable Development held in Johannesburg in 2002 (see Gorringe 2006:109). But there was still a keen sense in which the industry faces almost impossible economic pressures from markets to governmental author-ities. Could it be that such communities could find inspiration in Moxnes's reading of Jesus' exorcisms as symbolic of protest and empowerment on the part of those from below? Commentators fre-quently highlight that the term used to 'rebuke' the sea is more com-monly used in exorcism traditions. As such, Moxnes writes, 'since he and his followers combined exorcisms with the proclamation of the Kingdom, Jesus presented a different form of domination and control of space' (2003:138). Jesus' challenging of social, political and economic powers that destroy human flourishing on land can also be translated to marine environments. Those alien political forces that literally 'rock the boat' in coastal communities are accordingly contested.

The final biblical story on displacement (Luke 9.46–52) was re-flected on by the youth dance group that met in the centre. The small child who is symbolic of the ideal disposition of the disciple was chosen to choreograph a street dance in reference to the 'Son of Man having nowhere to lay his head'. The youngest person would lead the older ones, despite the initial difficulties in taking orders from the smallest. The group planned to perform a street dance in various parts of Newlyn where they felt physically displaced, including the disused quarry, the 'polite' residential area where they sometimes felt they were viewed with suspicion, and the centre of town itself. Often drama can play a part in heightening place sensitivities. The physical dance of these young people (akin to the performances of the Dalit and African interpreters outlined in Chapter 2) seemed to be one way to facilitate young people's reflection on place attachments and to effect a kind of physical displacement that may allow them to develop a wider sense of their location.

Newlyn: fishing for 'place'

As outlined in Chapter 1, in Western contexts, 'place amnesia' is a threat, with the bonds between topography, locality and people being increasingly threatened by advanced technology and mobility. The 'disengaged' and 'universal' increasingly eclipse the 'vernacular' and 'particular'. Despite this bleak picture, as G. Brent Ingram *et al.* have argued, there are still resistant 'places' in postmodernity, places which seek to cultivate relationships between people and land and which can act as models for contemporary place-making. In his words, 'though it may seem that cyberspace is outpacing physical space as a locus for social and cultural interaction, the role of the real, physical, public space is actually increasing for some kinds of contact' (Brent Ingram *et al.* 1997:4). While Western cultures may not always have exhibited such intense relationships with natural land-scapes as non-Western cultures, Elizabeth Bird reminds us these too 'are possessed by the need to turn spatial features into something that has meaning through narrative. We re-create place through historical reconstructions; we tell stories to locate us, where we feel we should be' (Bird 2002:523). In many ways Newlyn constitutes an example of what Brent Ingram *et al.* deemed a 'resistant place'. In various recent developments, particularly the Trinity project, Newlyn has sought to retain and celebrate local identities and avoid standardized, disengaged manifestations of community or 'heritage' pictures of Cornwall to be consumed by tourists. Indeed the very industry of fishing that formed the context for the group seemed to have symbolically informed the spirit of this regeneration plan. Fishing taught profound place-making tools. Fishing communities know the importance of navigating their ocean terrain (currents and reefs etc.) (Acheson 1981:291); so too those who seek to construct place need an in-depth knowledge of their physical place. Second, fishers need to know the habits of the fish they seek, their breeding and feeding patterns. Similarly place-makers need to chart all those 'out of place' (youth, homeless, those who don't attend particular community events etc.) and start to engage with their life-patterns if a place is to be truly inclusive.

The particular ways in which stories and coastal landscapes are connected, in Newlyn, are not static but rather in dynamic process, being actively reinterpreted and 'sensuously embodied in a multitude of ways' (Tilley 2006:8). As I observed in the Contextual Bible Study process, water and seas have profound metaphoric qualities. They can speak to communities about 'transmutability and fluidity; transformation, mood and movement' (Strang 2004:61). The sea likewise plays a part 'in a larger process of regeneration integral to a cycle of death, dissolution, reintegration and renewal' (Strang 2004:62). Unpredictable powers and their consequent threat to human flourishing were themes in the biblical stories and themes that were readily transplanted and adopted in the construction of 'place' by those in Newlyn participating in this study. Like the disciples on Lake Galilee, in Newlyn, 'the boat', 'the journey to the other side', 'the sea and storm' and 'the sailors' provided not only powerful commentaries on present collective identity but also potent stimuli for the future visions of the 'word in their place'.

7

Reading among the Deaf *

The most stringent power we have over another is not physical coercion but the ability to have the other accept our definition of them.

Stanley Hauerwas

The Deaf are, in a sense, racialised through their use of sign language as a system of communication . . . ghettoised as outsiders.

Lennard Davis

In recent years bodily discourses have raised interpreters' awareness of the means by which the 'able' or 'normal' are conceptualized in distinction to the 'disabled' or 'abnormal'. With these developments has come increased sensitivity to how biblical images of disability 'provide a window into a dynamic interchange between culture, author, text and audience' (Avalos, Melcher and Schipper 2007:5). Hector Avalos, for example, has developed 'sensory criticism' (Avalos 2007:51), which seeks to plot ways in which biblical texts evaluate senses, and how these may contribute to various ideological standpoints. Such perspectives allow biblical interpreters 'to gain a better appreciation of how biblical authors conceptualise and treat human embodiment' (Avalos 2007:58). Senses are entwined with social, literary, political and theological agendas. In his study, for example, Avalos contends that the Deuteronomic history promotes a sustained 'sonic theology', perhaps because covenants in the Ancient Near East were usually 'heard'. Yahweh is accordingly 'heard' by the people, but not seen. In contrast, the book of Job is identified as 'visiocentric', metaphors of sight and blindness pepper the text and the declaration in Job 42.5 highlights the superiority of visual encounters over auditory ones: 'I had heard of you by the hearing of

---

* A note on language: 'Deaf with capital D refers to culturally deaf people'; 'deaf with lower-case d refers to anyone with significant hearing loss'. 'Deaf mute' is no longer acceptable, rather 'd/Deaf people without speech' is preferred (see Lewis 2007:x). Hereafter I will capitalize Deaf to denote the cultural model of deafness.

91

the ear, but now my eyes see you.' Avalos rightly asserts that due to the historical ideologies 'sensory' criticism exposes, biblical interpreters are to be dissuaded from ever using such texts as vehicles to identify 'any particular view of the senses in biblical authors as "normative" [for] today' (Avalos 2007:59).

Despite Avalos's warning, many disability perspectives centred on the senses have started to approach biblical texts with both reading strategies of 'resistance' and 'recovery'. The 'resistance' approach views references to sensory impairment in biblical texts with suspicion and attempts to unmask the power structures that label one as 'disabled'. Reading strategies of 'recovery' seek to apologetically rehabilitate and rescue positive images of disability from the text (see especially John Hull's study on blindness, 2001). Even a cursory look at the New Testament in reference to 'sonic' themes reveals a cacophony of 'aural' imagery and thus a suspicion that the text 'disables' the full participation of the Deaf community within its discourses. Hearing a person's voice involves establishing a personal connection with him or her (the sheep know their own shepherd's voice in John 10.16). Moreover, the Johannine 'Word' declares 'Everyone who is of the truth hears my voice' (John 18.37). Similarly, God's revelations are primarily auditory, as at the baptism (Mark 1.11//Matt. 3.17//Luke 3.22), transfiguration (Mark 9.7//Matt. 17.5// Luke 9.35) and Paul's dramatic conversion (Acts 9.4). The faculty of hearing and the organ of the ear also become symbolic of cognition and insight: 'true hearing involves listening and understanding', thus 'to have deaf, heavy, or uncircumcised ears is to reject what is heard' (Ryken *et al.* 1998:223). As such, 'deafness' becomes a metaphor for misunderstanding: 'This is why I speak to them in parables . . . hearing they do not hear, nor do they understand' (Matt. 13.13).

Strategies of Deaf recovery could identify the fact that symbolic healing of blindness (and the concomitant spiritual 'enlightenment' that is often presupposed in the narration of such healings) takes a greater role within the Gospels than the healing of deafness. Indeed we only encounter one extended narrative of a healing of a deaf man in the Gospels (Mark 7.32ff.). In this episode Jesus puts his fingers in the man's ears, spits and touches his tongue (verse 33) and looking up to heaven demands that his ears be opened. Resistant readers could legitimately declare that this narrative follows a familiar 'oppressive' pattern of portraying characters with sensory impairment as nothing more than sites of divine action, 'objectified beneficiaries of divine healing' (Fontaine 1996, cited in Donaldson 2005:101), or more starkly in Nancy Eiesland's terms 'defiled evildoer[s]' (1994:70) in need of physical and spiritual 'wholeness'. Readings of a recovery nature, however, could possibly point to the fact that the 'Deaf' man was not pre-lingual Deaf, for Mark tells us that when his 'ears are opened, his tongue released, *he spoke plainly*' (Mark 7.35) (a person Deaf from birth would be without 'plain' speech, having never heard it). Recovery readings may also focus on positive images of 'light' (Matt. 4.16) and 'face' within the biblical tradition (Num. 6.25), for signing is a face-to-face performance and cannot be 'seen in the dark'.

Undoubtedly resisting oppressive ideologies of the senses and reconstructing biblical texts more positively in sensory terms is an important part of liberating 'disability' readings. Generally, though, it is true to say that 'sensory' surveys of biblical texts, especially when disability is so often used metaphorically for social commentary and critique, do not really focus on the real 'lived experience of disability' (Schipper 2007:103). It is this lacuna that I seek to address here by engaging with contemporary Deaf readers in the Contextual Bible Study process.

The Deaf: a community of shared experience

Nearly 9 million people in the UK have hearing impairments (Lees 2007:166). However, by no means all of those people would consider themselves Deaf with a capital 'D', or be regarded as such by the Deaf community. It is important at the outset to clarify what we mean when we talk about the Deaf. This inevitably affects different models of 'deafness' held within discourse. The 'medical' model sees the inability to hear as impairment and one that can be overcome to some degree by the use of hearing aids or implants. The field of Disability Studies, however, has set out to question essentialist categorizations of disability and has redefined it as a 'form of social oppression, inequality and exclusion' (see Hutchinson 2006:2). The alternative 'socio-cultural' perspective they propose sees the physical or social environment in which the person lives as 'disabling'. It is the third model, however, that encapsulates Deaf with a capital 'D' most appropriately, namely the cultural perspective. This sees the Deaf as a minority language group rather than a people who cannot hear properly and it is this understanding that informed Kyle and Woll's definition of the Deaf community in their celebrated volume on *Sign Language* (1988):

> It involves a shared language; it involves hearing loss; it involves social interaction and politics . . . but all of these interrelate and interact with attitudes towards other Deaf people. The choice to communicate and share information with other people must be seen as a primary feature, and because of the language used by members of the community this communication will generally be restricted to other Deaf people. (Kyle and Woll 1988:5)

Hannah Lewis contends that historical instances of the disempowerment of the Deaf (particularly with reference to their own language) are analogous to political colonization defined as 'a process of physical subjugation, imprisonment of an alien language, culture and mores and the regulation of education on behalf of colonial goals' (Lewis 2007:32). Following this line of thinking Roger Hitching (2003:16) pinpoints, within the field of Deaf education, a significant date for such colonization as being the 1880 Milan Congress where, in his words, 'a small group of paternalistic hearing instructors opposed to the use of sign language decided that it would be in the best interests of Deaf people if teachers adopted oralism' and actively suppressed the use of sign language (Hitching 2003:16). Thus oralism (an ideology which devalues sign language and espoused oral methods of education with lip-reading as central) became a colonial tool, forcedly imposing the 'spoken word' on the Deaf community. The Milan Congress has since been identified in much of the literature as the single most important event for driving sign language underground and limiting not only the education and literacy of many Deaf children but also the decline of Deaf culture itself.

The educational context was not alone in promoting colonization of Deaf culture. Missions to Deaf people founded in the late nineteenth century likewise opposed and vetoed the use of sign language. 'Hearing' missioners tried to educate with a strong dose of patriarchal paternalism and as such 'seemed to be carrying out a form of cultural imperialism as much as they were spreading the gospel'

(Hitching 2003:23). The paternalistic rhetoric evident in both the educational and missionary contexts constructed Deaf people as passive and dependent. Indeed the sentiments contained in the 1993 Church of England report, *The Church among Deaf People*, could well have been written by one of those paternalistic Victorian missionaries that Hitching finds so objectionable. It condescendingly states:

> Their [the Deaf's] relationship with God, and his with them, is often untrammelled by detail or the complexities of knowledge and understanding. Often their faith is direct, clear and simple, but very powerful because it feels, to those who knew them, like the faith Jesus calls for, the faith that is childlike in its openness and trust.
>
> (Church of England 1997:60–1)

As a result of these dynamics, Davis and others have drawn comparisons between stigmatization of the colonized and the Deaf (see Davis 1995:78). Reacting to these oppressive trends, the 1970s witnessed the rise of the Deaf Pride movement. Deaf Pride involved a recovery of lost (literally silenced) moments of Deaf history and British Sign Language was at last recognized as a discrete language with its own structure, grammar and regional variations (see Lewis 2007:26). This led to the development of cultural dynamics of 'Deaf World' and 'Deaf Way' ('an abstraction for imagining the social identity and cultural milieus that Deaf people can share' (Senghas and Monaghan 2002:80)) where sign language was freely used (Lewis 2007:22). The colonized were at last openly resisting the oppressive structures that had previously 'silenced' them. The accessibility (or rather inaccessibility) of texts within BSL has, though, continued to perpetuate an 'outsider' status, even in times of Deaf Pride. While the works of Shakespeare are in part now available in BSL, the Bible still is not (although a BSL version is currently being produced and this will ease the situation considerably). One member of the group I worked with signed, 'Deaf people have no access to the Bible. It's very hard, even in a Deaf church, to read the Bible at the same time that someone is signing it. One big advantage of technology is that in the future we will have access to the Bible in BSL straight to our iPods that will mean that Deaf people will feel more confident because they will have already seen the Bible in Sign.'

Contextual readings among the Deaf

It was important at the outset that the group was allowed open access to all materials in BSL and that an appropriate 'Deaf Space' was created. As with other cultural minorities who do not have a Bible openly accessible to them in their own language, even introducing the text to the group involved complex considerations. I was advised against using Sign Supported English (SSE), which follows English word order and finger spells some of the terms, as this is quite hard to understand in reference to biblical stories: 'SSE translations are fraught with conflicts, aberrations and ambivalences, usually unintelligible and onerous to the majority of Deaf people' (Lewis 2007:115). It was suggested that it would be better to give the texts in English (for the benefit of those members who could read) but also that a group member should tell the story in BSL (for the benefit of *all*, both readers and non-readers within the group). Telling stories in BSL, as I learned, was to engage with a performative and collective culture that envisaged the group not primarily as 'readers' but 'retellers' (Lees 2007:166). 'Remembered Bible' is a term that Gerald West has used in reference to communal conceptions of a story (West 1996, cited in Lees 2007:163) as opposed to literalistic renderings, and this seems to have resonance with the BSL readings offered in my study.

In their reading of the first story (Luke 15.11–32) and reflections on the idea of home, the group first interpreted the characters within the story as Deaf, the younger son however wanted to leave the Deaf community and interact with the hearing world. As conversation went on, another interpretation was offered: the youngest son was a (hearing) CODA (child of deaf adults). He had grown up within a family and acted as interpreter for his parents. In a sense, he felt abused, his own goals and ambitions could not be realized due to his interpreting responsibilities, and as a result he decided to leave home. The father's welcome home therefore was not to a wayward son, but rather to someone who had resisted oppressive forces imposed upon him and also someone who had eventually come to accept his basic identity and acknowledge his home place, though hearing, within Deaf culture. This stimulated yet another reading: the younger son could be the deaf child of hearing parents who decided to leave his family to go to the Deaf community. This raised some interesting observations on the power assumptions inherent within the text itself that labelled the 'Deaf' world as a place of dissolute living, impurity and famine (verses 13–14). The punchline of the story, however, involves the Deaf child returning to his hearing family and the family as a result making a great effort to learn sign language (exemplified by the killing of the fatted calf and ring and sandals) so the child would feel 'in place'. Yet another reading saw the younger son being given a second chance. He represented, in one participant's words:

> Deaf people at school who are educated through a variety of methods including oralism; when they grow up and leave school they often shun the Deaf community. They immerse themselves in the hearing world, form relationships and even marry hearing people but all the time something is missing inside themselves: the language and culture of the community is what's missing. When the Deaf community accepts them back it's like a second chance – like the son who was 'dead' and now is alive.

Related to this, another participant thought that Deaf people (imaged in the lost son) may think that the world of the hearing has everything. They may go in search of this world, but in the end find it wanting – 'They may look rich, but do they hold language and culture dear to their hearts?' – and have to return home to the Deaf space where community is central. In one participant's view, 'Whereas here in the Deaf world we may look poor, we are so rich because of our language and culture, so to my mind it goes back to values – the values we have, the riches we hold are those that will last – more like the values of heaven.'

There were instances, however, where tensions between concepts inherent within the story and the visual translation into sign language surfaced. One particularly insightful example of this identified by one participant involved reflection on the signing of the word 'forgive' that the BSL version of the story presented to the group had used. The sign for 'forgive' evokes the meaning of making the slate clean. Accordingly the participant stated:

> There's a lot of debate about how we should translate that word into Sign Language. There's an idea that it should be a fixed sign – forgive – as in wiping away all sin. I don't think it should be. The elder brother clearly didn't want his brother back, but the father accepted

him back and was prepared to move on. This is forgiveness. The signs we use should show acceptance and moving on. He accepted that the son was back and he was prepared to move on. But the older son had the old idea of forgiveness – of wiping the slate clean and he wouldn't do it. That's the problem today – a lot of people have that idea about forgiveness. But really it means that you can say to a person, 'OK I know you did things in the past that were wrong. I accept that, and we're ready to move on. I won't look back, we'll move on!'

In the original Greek, we are told that the father did not literally 'forgive' (though his behaviour could perhaps be legitimately interpreted in that way) but rather was filled with 'compassion' or 'pity'. His actions – seeing, holding and kissing – illustrate the acceptance and moving on of which the participant spoke. The elder son by contrast does seem, as the Deaf interpreter suggests, to work more with the idea of forgiveness as 'wiping the slate clean', which, in the end, he cannot bring himself to do: 'but it is possible that, out of love and respect for his father, he will [eventually] be persuaded by his father's words' (Tannehill 1996:244). In effect this Deaf reader had touched upon the central crux of the parable: 'The story of the prodigal supports the remarkable connection in Luke between repentance and joy . . . the sign of repentance is not fasting and mourning but joy demonstrated in communal celebration; in the prodigal son, this celebration is preceded by the son's return home and confession' (Tannehill 1996:242).

The second story, the boy Jesus in the temple (Luke 2.41–52), provoked more reflections on the themes of being 'home'. The group was struck by the seeming comfortableness of the boy Jesus in the temple, even though to the teachers of the law he must have seemed 'out of place'. One participant remarked: 'The temple was his place . . . a bit like the Deaf club for us. I wouldn't say "Oh I'm off to the Deaf club for a while, you don't mind do you?" I would just go.' Another shared the story of a Deaf priest who, in theological college, would sneak out to visit the local Deaf club. The priest thought the bishop did not know about these secret excursions, but actually he did know about them all along: 'He was amazed since he assumed that if anyone had caught him he would have been punished or thrown out of the seminary but he wasn't, the bishop let him go to the Deaf community'. Another spoke about the fact that Jesus may have felt 'out of place' within his own family unit and therefore sought solace in the temple, a place he felt more comfortable with. In response to this, others shared experiences about missing family occasions (birthdays and weddings) in order to attend Deaf club functions that were scheduled for the same day. It was incredible how time and again the image of the temple in the story became symbolic of the Deaf club, a place where the group felt 'in place'. 'Normal' churches were seen as those arenas in which the participants felt 'out of place': 'deaf people need to sit in circles to discuss stuff . . . "hearing" churches are arranged with rows of pews'; 'the thing that makes me feel remote from church is all that singing, it does not mean anything to us'; 'I was invited to a "healing" service, my friend insisted that I go out the front for prayer. The guy prayed for me and tried his best to make me hear but nothing happened. I received nothing! Personally I think God wants me to remain Deaf.'

All participants with their diverse retellings highlighted for me the redundancies and gaps within the English translations of the biblical stories, which BSL, as a primarily visual, spatial and performative language, 'filled in'. Each retelling, even if broadly based on the English text, involved some additional details that fleshed out the story 'visually' in the mind's eye. The signing of our third biblical story by one participant in the group, the stilling of the storm (Luke 8.22–39), illustrates just this. Translated from BSL, this individual's 'retelling' reads as follows:

Jesus had been preaching and teaching and now wanted to rest. He decided they should go back to the other side of the lake so he asked Peter to do him a favour and take him across the lake in the boat. Peter called his other friends to set to work and they all got into the boat. They hoisted the sail and pushed off from the shore. Very soon, Jesus fell fast asleep because he was so tired. The disciples hard at work in the boat noticed that he was asleep and agreed to leave him since he was so tired. They continued their sail across the lake. A little later the water became a bit choppy and the boat started to toss. The weather got worse and worse until the waves were huge and the little boat was in danger of being swamped. Meanwhile Jesus was still fast asleep (and snoring) in the back of the boat. The disciples really wanted to wake him up but they felt they shouldn't. They discussed it among themselves. They said that the wind was so bad and the waves so high there was real danger so he should wake up. How could they get out of danger? The disciples argued about who should wake up Jesus since none of them wanted to. One said, 'I can't reach him, I'm too busy trying to steer a straight course.' One of the men was too scared to touch Jesus. Eventually one person woke him up and said that all the crew was frightened of drowning because it was so rough. Jesus stood up in the boat and told the wind and waves to calm down. The water immediately calmed down. All the disciples were utterly amazed. 'That's fantastic', they said. 'How did he do that?' 'Ah well,' said another, 'he is Jesus after all – that's God!' Jesus said to them all, 'Where's your faith?' Immediately they started defending themselves and blaming each other for their fear. In the end they said, 'How did he do that? He really is God's Son.'

The journey being conceived as a journey 'back' across the lake (rather than to alien territory on the other side); the disciples leaving Jesus alone because he was tired; the hoisting of the sail; their hard work; Jesus' snoring; the disciples' arguments about who was going to wake Jesus up; the question about *how* Jesus accomplished the stilling of the water (as opposed to Luke's identity question of 'Who then is this that even the winds and waves obey him?') – all these things visually enriched, and in parts changed, the depiction of the story. That 'sign language seeks to involve the person being signed to in the reliving of the story, which is the container for the information being conveyed' (Hitching 2003:43), certainly seems to have been corroborated here. The group imagined themselves as crew on the boat and pictured the chaotic sea as the government's policies on Deaf education literally tossing the boat of their community. One participant noted:

> We know today that a lot of Deaf schools are closing and we understand that one of the reasons is that it's too expensive for Local Authorities to send Deaf children to residential Deaf schools, but the expense is nothing compared to the wealth the children gain as they experience language and community. We share community experience in the same way that God wants us to share his community experience and his love.

Another imagined the journey to the other side of the lake as a Federation for Deaf People rally, sailing together to London to campaign for the recognition of BSL as a language in its own right. Legion was seen as a figure that offended the 'tyranny of normality' (Hauerwas 2004:37–43). His isolation was perhaps not only on account of his being an outcast, but also a self-imposed preservation mechanism against the pain of being rendered 'abnormal'; until one is empowered and welcomed to interact with other people, it is easier as a 'dis-abled' person just to associate with oneself or others like oneself.

The final story, being a series of sayings rather than a narrative, seemed harder for a 'retelling' in BSL. We therefore spoke in more general terms about displacement. The group considered this theme in relation to those 'outside' the Deaf community who seemed to lack the know-how of true communion with the Deaf. The fact that 'normal' hearing church was viewed as an inhospitable place offered a strong agenda for change. This group of interpreters visualized the fact that 'wholeness is not the product of self-sufficiency or inter-dependence but rather of the genuinely inclusive community that results from sharing our humanity with one another in light of the grace of God' (Reynolds 2008:18). The Deaf readers did construct themselves as an isolated community – separated from others on account of their experience – but who over and again were forced to assimilate and try to engage with the hearing world. Their plea for 'hands to the plough' seems to be one that made the hearing world take similar steps to engage and understand Deaf way and Deaf world.

A signs source

Given that some Deaf people, especially from the older generation, cannot read, biblical studies and other 'industries' of the book have promoted hegemonic 'textual' discourses that have marginalized them and their language. One of the great contributions of post-modernism has been to acknowledge and celebrate diverse forms and media of knowledge. To give just one example, reading with sub-alterns in India (Dalit peoples etc.) Sathianathan Clarke has com-mended a 'multimodal' approach that encourages oppressed groups to 'perform' transformation in response to biblical narrative and images. In oral cultures interpretations are 'corporately weaved to-gether' (Clarke 2002:262) and frequently represented in 'media other than writing' (Clarke 2002:263); the Dalits for instance use drumming, dancing, spinning, weaving, painting and carving in their hermeneu-tics. Clarke urges mainstream biblical studies literally to 'come to its senses' and acknowledge the great contribution cultures that speak with their hands, rather than words and written texts, can offer:

> It is pertinent to register the point that communities that work with their hands and are intimately related to the products they create do not have a need to separate reflective activity from the material activity they are involved with. Thus production, reflection and communication are connected and integrated into a human way of living. Praxis is a way of life.   (Clarke 2002:264)

In a similar vein the postcolonial feminist Musa Dube initiates contextual interpretations of biblical stories among African readers and revels in the dictum offered by one participant that 'God never opened the Bible'. This graphically illustrates the fact that God was active and dynamic, not contained in, or contained by, particular written directives in printed texts. Dube accordingly celebrates those, like the Deaf community, who 'retell and weave their own stories of healing and empowerment' (Dube 2000:195). In relation to Deaf biblical interpretation sign language as a medium needs to be valued, not only for the great contribution it makes in visualizing the biblical texts – how was the sail hoisted on boats in first-century Galilee? – but also as a representative language of an oral culture. Sign language in itself is a mode of communication in a collective culture and as such may be nearer the earliest Palestinian 'oral' modes of transmission of 'gospel' traditions. Richard Bauckham's recent work on the oral transmission of gospel traditions has, for example, attempted to expose the fallacy of seeing oral traditions being passed within communities in an anonymous, dispassionate way. Bauckham adopts Samuel Byrskog's work which compares the practices of Graeco-Roman historians with contemporary 'oral history' and links this with Loveday Alexander's claim that the 'living voice' operated in rhetoric to underline the importance of live performance: among craftspeople to demonstrate that one cannot learn without live demonstrations and in schools where person-to-person communication was rated above study of books or manuals (see Bauckham 2003:29, 37). Similarly within Deaf culture, face-to-face performance through sign is valued over and above static traditions or words. Galen's dictum, which praises and values those dynamic and transformative face-to-face encounters above 'those who navigate out of books' (see Bauckham 2003:37), may provide some cultural comparisons with collective oral traditions.

In a similar vein S. Tyler has recently petitioned us to literally '*de-scribe*', resist the limiting power structures of the written word, for in his opinion such moves stultify the possibilities of the imagination: 'writing puts everything in the past, it has no future'; 'The past is the incurable illness of writing' (Tyler 1986:135). He submits that oral cultures provide a resistance to this 'algebraism – shufflings of meaningless signs'. In his opinion 'our redemption in/from this tale of loss and liberation is not in sight nor in hand [by which he means scribal practice] could it be just on the tips of our tongues? [or more specifically in the actions of our hands in sign]?' (Tyler 1986:137). As such a 'signs source' could be pregnant with promise for imagining new avenues of creativity.

Oral and performative cultures are collective as opposed to individualistic and as such 'oral hermeneutics' often appropriates a text to a cultural context shared by others: 'Sometimes the story is framed in a new context, or the ending changed, or variants suggested alongside the original story' (Lewis 2007:120). Paddy Ladd likewise claims that storytelling is central to Deaf identity and is one of the primary means by which Deaf experience can be transformed from the margin to the centre, to reclaim narratives from the past and alleviate dissonance between history and contemporary life. He suggests that 'storytelling is a form of oral transmission of text, it is a traditional art in many cultures, including Deaf culture, and in the hands of a skilled practitioner accurately transmits what is seen as the essence of the narrative' (Ladd 2003, discussed in Lewis 2007:118). Unlike in Luke's original version of the stilling of the storm narrative where the characters remain bemused about Jesus' identity ('Who then is this that the winds and the waves obey him?'), in the 'performance' of the story the end becomes a 'gestic' declaration of faith to the community: 'How did he do that?' 'Ah well,' said another, 'He is Jesus after all – that's God!' The attitudes of the characters and the storyteller become important parts of the reading: in Hitching's terms such interpretations are not merely giving the meaning 'but also the speaker's attitude to his listeners and to what he is saying' (Hitching 2003:70) within the performance. To this end, Peter McDonough's study of issues of translation of gospel stories into sign language found that what the Deaf community and the hearing community valued as good translations differed significantly. For the Deaf, the most important criteria were that translations were 'embodied in [their] own culture and colloquial idiom'. In contrast, for the hearing the most important element was a 'direct and true translation of biblical texts' (McDonough 1998, discussed in Lewis 2007:118).

Lewis, in her recent steps towards the construction of Deaf liberation theology (2007), brings out the importance of contextual readings by the Deaf quite forcefully when she openly states: 'I am not really interested in what hearing people, however involved with Deaf people they might be, have said about what Deaf people think and what a theology of the Deaf would look like!' (Lewis 2007:6). The import of her claim is that the 'hearing' foreigners need to take careful notice of what the Deaf community's 'signs source' on its own terms has to teach us. While it is possible to revisit 'sensory' images within biblical texts to recover or resist certain portrayals, here, by reading with the Deaf community, I have sought to engage with the 'lived experience' of Deafness. I have proposed that a Deaf biblical interpretation constitutes a challenge to the hegemony of written texts and in common with other performative interpretations advocates multimodal forms of interpretation. To use Hitching's particularly evocative image, Deaf hermeneutics 'moves away from a purely wordy God to one in terms of vision and touch . . . A God who gives visions and dreams' (Hitching 2003:21). In order to challenge textual hegemony one must, as Lennard Davis contends, not only make 'Deafness' more 'mainstream', but also reconstruct the centre to become more 'Deaf-stream'. In his words, 'one of the tasks for a developing consciousness of disability issues is the attempt, then, to reverse the hegemony of the normal and to institute alternative ways of thinking about the [normal and] abnormal' (Davis 1995:49). This is surely at the centre of a gospel message that 'displaces economies of exchange based in the cult of normalcy' (Reynolds 2008:249). Contextual studies could be not only the start of a remembrance of Deaf history in the Bible but also a challenge to those hearers who as yet 'do not have ears to hear' the potential contribution of the Deaf-way in the construction of a truly inclusive place.

8

Reading among the clergy

Authorized ministers represent the people of God and have no existence independent of the rest of the Body of Christ. The priest is no more the Church than the Prime Minister is Great Britain.

John Pritchard

Clergy are in effect a 'professional class', educated and trained to teach and preach scriptures to others. For this reason this particular interpretative group stands apart from the 'folk' interpretations presented hitherto. In the contextualizing of biblical stories within both their vocations and the communities in which they serve, the clergy were encouraged to experience a democratic and participatory mode of biblical interpretation that they could subsequently use among lay groups in their own contexts. In such a process their position would be transformed in the perceptions of the group from 'clergy' (power role) to 'person' (one voice among many in an egalitarian group). Of course, promotion of this type of thinking strikes a ready chord with reforms in theological education in the last decade. Christian ministry is increasingly advocating 'facilitation' *of* others rather than 'expertise' *over* others. As such, 'theological discourse is now seen as process rather than product . . . [enabling] people of faith to give account of the values and traditions that underpin their choices and convictions and deepen their understanding' (Graham, Walton and Ward 2005:5–6). The *Hind Report*, commissioned by the Archbishops' Council, has promoted the 'learning church' model to demonstrate just this. Formation is relevant not just to clergy, but all Christian people, for 'theology is vital for every Christian, and even though clergy might be expected to be theologians, theirs is not a professionalism that belongs to them alone' (*Hind Report* 2003:27). The goal of theological education is, according to the report, 'inhabited wisdom', which comprises 'immersion in scripture' and an active response 'to the issues of present-day life' (*Hind Report* 2003:42). In order to foster such awareness, the report underlines the importance of the development of cultural sensitivities among those serving as clergy, for 'Christian apologetics as well as social engagement requires ministers who are versatile to "read the signs of the times"' (*Hind Report* 2003:29). It seems that such goals resonate with the mobilization of civic responsibility, social capital and reflection on the part of church communities in effecting social transformation. It also has deep connections with the Contextual Bible Study rationale in constructing and valuing a community in which diverse voices are heard and acted upon.

In New Testament literature the conception of learning and growing among a 'priesthood of all believers' is of course well documented (Heb. 9.14; Rom. 12.1), as is the corporate, interdependent structure of the body of Christ (Rom. 12.5–8) and the collective 'building' of the community (1 Cor. 3.10–15). *Koinōnia* (communion and fellowship) lies at the heart of the New Testament ideal of the Church as a dynamic, living organism, made up of diverse and interdependent parts. Of no minor consequence in this light is the fact that Jesus' own movement seems in places to have been ambivalent, even opposed to traditional, Jewish authority structures ('anti-clerical'). The Kingdom is not established within the sacred power structures of the day and its central space of the temple; rather, the domestic space of the house becomes symbolic of a Kingdom built on relationships rather than hierarchical roles. Jesus' *lay* charismatic leadership is demonstrated not in cultic ritual but communal feasting, being with life's nuisances and nobodies and, as a servant, washing the feet of others. Only in the letter to the Hebrews is Christ portrayed as the 'great high priest' who offers himself as the once-and-for-all sacrifice, yet even here his great gift of self-giving is a radical sacrifice for the advantage of others. Modelled on Christ's example, then, servant-hood and 'being alongside' others through various experiences seems to be the central essence of New Testament conceptions of ministry.

In place terms the ministry model promoted in the Jesus movement is one of 'a wandering itinerancy'. The mission call charges followers to leave home, family, belongings and livelihoods to evangelize, preach and concretely demonstrate the Kingdom in action through poverty and trust in God to provide (Mark 6.6–13 etc.). As the Church institutionalized, assimilation to the status quo occurred and more formal structures of leadership seem to have been instituted (1 Tim. 3). The ideal of the 'wandering' charismatic, though, is still suggestive for the picture of ministry today. Ministers are called to work within the community but also to remain to some extent 'outside' of it. Like an anthropologist going to study an alien people, their ministry has 'insider/participant' dimensions and 'outsider/observer' dimensions in order that perspective can be gained on the people. One needs a certain amount of detachment to act as a prophet, a herald of change and voice of conscience within communities, for the clergy 'may be called on by the gospel to take a stand against a clear injustice or an ethically dubious action' (Pritchard 2007:91). But at the same time clergy must immerse themselves in local cultures in order to provide a critique which 'comes from within rather than be imposed from outside' (Gibbs and Bolger 2006:16). To read and construct 'place' with clergy, therefore, involves reflecting on 'inherited models' but also hopefully imagining 'fresh expressions' of ministry in contemporary mixed economies of church and culture and ordained and lay responsibilities (Pritchard 2007:xi).

Contextual readings from clergy

The evidence presented here is a synthesis of responses to the biblical stories collected at clergy conferences (URC and Anglican respectively). Pursuing one strand of current Fresh Expressions/Emerging Church thinking (alternative forms of church within postmodern culture) the primary aim of these events was to explore ways of encouraging clergy to engage in theological reflection on the biblical stories and to present findings in creative multi-modal pursuits (drawing, painting, drama, dance, song-writing etc.). Through Contextual Bible Study ministers were invited to image and contextualize the biblical stories, and then engage in artistic workshops (facilitated by specialized artists etc.) which would reflect their feelings about the biblical stories expressed through creative media. The image of 'artist' was threaded throughout the events with God presupposed as the archetypal artist who invites all people to 'paint'. Clergy accordingly were posited as 'conveners of the painting workshop' within their own contexts, not due to their superior art skills but rather simply that they were called to this service. John Pritchard continues the art analogy when he states:

> And so we get on with the great commission, not 'painting by numbers' but rather 'painting after the style of Christ' – that artist's equally gifted Son. In every church in the world, in every locality and in each life, the painting goes on. (Pritchard 2007:7)

The first 'artworks' for consideration from scripture were the images of home and journeying as encountered in the parable of the lost son (Luke 15.11–32). The groups began by sharing objects that they would later artistically represent, which summed up their place as home. One participant, who brought a rotting apple from an orchard adjoining the church grounds, saw within this object a parable of the church as the place where creation and fall were dramatized; but through a community built around a common table in Eucharist, redemption was also part of the story he felt called to proclaim. Another participant openly shared his exhaustion with the trials of ministry imaged in a 'Flora margarine pot' which he felt summed up his frequent feelings of being 'low on fat and very thinly spread!' Another from a church on the Jurassic coast brought a fossil: he saw the erosion of limestone cliffs as analogous to the erosion of his church community. Doggedly to resist change held the threat of the Church becoming 'fossilized'. He feared that talk of fresh expressions belied the fact that the Church was perceived to be stale and past its best. The challenge of ministry in such a context was great.

With these images in mind, many participants in the groups primarily (and surprisingly) identified with the lost son within the parable. They witnessed that clergy 'are almost bound at some stage to encounter periods of sheer emotional and spiritual weariness' (Pritchard 2007:26), and to run away to a far-off country was an attractive possibility. Others read the parable as a fable against the fear of failure. The lost son headed out with dreams and visions, but when these came to nothing, he was still welcomed home. Much of the discussion of the groups centred on how society was obsessed with success; sometimes parents would 'adopt' success through their children's achievements, but the father in this story does not compel the son to *do* anything against his will, but rather allows him just to *be*. In this respect, as clergy, they felt that their communities should be encouraged in taking risks if that was their calling, firm in the knowledge that success would be celebrated and failure would be met with forgiveness and acceptance. However, it was also reasonable, like the constancy of the older son within the story, to remember, value and preserve tradition and the 'way things had been in the past', for this was an important vessel of God's presence within 'place'. The father in the story says as much when he declares to the elder son, 'you are always with me, and all that is mine is yours' (Luke 15.31).

The image of the father's home within the story was also understood as a powerful representation of the church as a place that develops 'self-worth' in all people and builds communities of repentance and forgiveness. One participant noted how a certain social dispute, which she did not elaborate on, had marred her church community for over thirty years. In a centenary writing project different people documented their own views on these events, allowing the story to be publicly recorded and heard from different viewpoints for the first time.

All in all, participants seemed to acknowledge that success and failure, adventure and constancy were inherent parts of ministry, but that none of these should be prized above another. Even failure should be accepted, for this keeps the reality of the clergy's limitations helpfully in focus; when things go wrong, they must exhibit the humility of the lost son, repent and ask for forgiveness safe in the knowledge that they will once again find a home. Moreover, the example of the father in the narrative encouraged the groups to ponder the need to give people the freedom to be expressive and do their own thing in the context of church, not holding them back but rather empowering them to explore avenues important to them; and in the end celebrating their successes and being there for them if things did not work out as planned. A generation conditioned never to fail, bred on the ideology of 'deferred success', was a generation that never encountered the true possibility of growth.

The next story, on the theme of those 'out of place' (Luke 2.41–52), saw the clergy more readily identifying with the parents and travelling community than the teachers of the law or the Christ child. The fact that it took three days for the parents to even notice Jesus' absence was likened by one participant to the plodding along with the normalities of ministry in blissful ignorance of more serious problems that lay beneath the surface. Others saw the church imaged in the travelling group, itself a community 'out of place' (a minority community) and noted the immense importance of the complete trust showed by the parents in the ability and care of the community. This was allegorized by other participants as the promotion and valuing of lay ministries within the church community: the parents (clergy) could not be expected to do everything, but they in turn needed to demonstrate confidence in the gifts of others.

In relation to this the travelling group was itself constructed as a 'place' even in its temporary 'displacement'. They had common stories and face-to-face interaction even if they were a pilgrim, journeying people. Like nomads, when camped for the night, this travelling group would have presumably offered hospitality and shared stories with one another. In essence the travelling group artistically presented the church as 'movement' rather than 'institution', a realization that was particularly redolent in the dance and drama seminars. It is perhaps no accident that the Greek term *ekklesia* also denotes movement rather than stillness: 'it refers to the calling out of a people . . . in its broader sense in the Roman city, it referred to a town meeting in a public place' (Gibbs and Bolger 2006:98). With this in mind the clergy pondered the fact that unlike temples (and many churches and heritage buildings) bodies move around and can travel great distances. Such movement affords much greater possibilities for 'place-making' than a static structure ever could. Another participant reflected pastorally on the torment of the parents; their story of temporary loss would have been rich and painful but it is not extensively elaborated on in scripture. The participant urged others in the group to seek out stories of pain within communities, for sharing tragedy and fear was central to overcoming fractures within family, church and community life.

Turning to the character of Jesus, some saw that the story undercuts the assumption that the world has the dominant role in forming the person or minister. The child Jesus had to be away from the world in order to allow him to explore the questions he wanted to. This 'being away' (outsider) and 'being with' (insider) in parallel were seen as crucial parts of ministry, for one needed to be perceived as both native (a solid part of the community) and prophet (one capable of initiating change within the community). Moreover, respite and retreat away from the community were also acknowledged as potent parts of clergy formation. The final reflection drew an analogy between the Contextual Bible Study process we were involved in and the fact that in the biblical story Jesus was listening *and* asking questions – he was in dialogue – he was not shut in an isolated office, but rather in dynamic conversation with others. This two-way process of scriptural understanding seemed a pertinent one in breaking the perception of clergy as a 'scribal' leadership rather than participants in the collective 'painting' of the relevance of scripture in a particular community.

The third story (Luke 8.22–39), on the stilling of the storm and the exorcism of Legion, saw, perhaps unsurprisingly, many participants pick up on the analogy of the church as a boat 'rocked by various cultural waves'. One participant rhetorically asked the others to consider what type of boat they felt they were riding in? A lifeboat which was sailing purposively to throw lines and lifejackets to the world outside, or a passenger ferry that merely picked up congregational passengers and dropped them off each Sunday? The narrative tells of happenings in the eye of a storm when 'the boat was filling with water'. Many saw that one has to acknowledge when one has reached the limits of competence within the ship of the church and turn to God in trust and prayer. Also one has to acknowledge that the power of the Spirit can itself not only be comforting but a disturbing power which challenges the church to leave its comfort zones. This led to a link with the Legion narrative, as another participant noted that the proverbial saying 'better the devil you know than the devil you don't' illustrates that people and communities can become comfortable with their demons, for it is less frightening to live alongside them than witness convulsing and violent exorcisms of past practice.

Another interesting observation on the boat analogy was the fact that the image of the 'contained' church in the ship could mean that interaction with outside agencies was not given the due attention it deserves. There is no energy to be with, or rooted with, agencies that are not church, but members spoke of very generative relationships that had been developed with, for example, the Youth Enquiry Service and Christian youth programmes. Indeed the former had tried to initiate a number of contacts with Christian communities to no avail, until they had established the link through this group participant. This led to further 'artistic' reflections on the story. One participant had brought a stone, which once formed part of a wall that had been demolished in the churchyard. She reflected on the fact

111

that while the church was built on rock, if such structures disallowed engagements with others, then walls needed to be dismantled to let outside activities and people in.

The fact that Legion was sent home following his exorcism and that the narrative reveals he went to the city proclaiming what God had done brought another iconic reflection of the church as 'organic plant' to mind. The participants spoke about the journeys taken by some in leaving a building that could not be financially sustained and literally replanting themselves in a community space (halls, schools etc.) where the church became symbolized not by bricks and mortar but by people. This creative use of space was seen to imaginatively grow new roots, or, to pick up on an image in the biblical story, new unified 'personalities' and allow a transformed church (physically and socially) 'clothed and in its right mind' to work among a wider cross-section of the people.

One particular insightful observation shared was the fact that peace and order within the story was given by the employment of authority. The disciples wondered at the authority of Jesus in silencing the stormy elements, and the demons were afraid of Jesus' power and authority: they asked for his permission to enter into the swine. In a culture where the mythology of freedom and personal choice is prized, the image of authority is frequently denigrated. However, as Richard Bauckham has noted, freedom is nurtured in relationships, not threatened by them. Thus the authority of God allows human creatures to exercise their own freedoms. In turn it encourages the Church and those who serve within it, not to be afraid to exercise authority and promote an alternative voice to the cultural pursuit of uncontrolled individualistic freedom:

> Freedom is not threatened by, but formed and nurtured by dependence, belonging, relationship and community and importantly and most controversially, authority . . . Only in a context of values and practices of life in which human life is related to God can such freedom be adequately sustained. (Bauckham 2002:3)

In quite the opposite extreme, others spoke of the over-dependency on and over-expectation of the clergy, displayed by some of their congregations. The double-edged sword of being a person who exercised authority was summed up in the response of one participant who declared, 'I wish the congregation would look at heaven and stop looking at me!' Pritchard sums up this wrong perception of the clergy frequently held in communities as 'superhero'. In his words, 'it is the exhausting joy and timeless privilege . . . to be the "presiding genius" as the church leans forward to meet her Lord with such exquisite intimacy' (Pritchard 2007:21).

The final narrative (Luke 9.46–52) produced three key reflections from the participants centred on the images of journey and destination, displacement and leading/following. Many participants picked up on the image of 'those that are not against us are for us' and related it to the fact that while less than 10 per cent of the population of Britain regularly attend church, 70 per cent acknowledge some belief in God. These participants outside traditional religious observance, in a so-called post-Christian age, should also be perceived as travellers on the journey of faith. Likewise the powerful image of 'leaving the dead to bury the dead' was seen to involve the honest acknowledgment that some ways of 'being church' in some contexts were outdated. It was no use going through the motions of 'dead theatre' week by week, 'embalming' outdated traditions and rituals. It was better to leave rotting practices and structures behind in search of radical new ways of embodying Kingdom within particular contexts.

The image of Jesus travelling through Samaritan territory en route to his own destination of the cross in Jerusalem led to the realization that his 'place' is not a final destination but rather a journey to radical homelessness. In Walter Brueggemann's terms, the cross denotes the image of God as most displaced:

> Thus crucifixion/resurrection echoes the dialectic of possessed land lost/exiles en route to the land of promise. Jesus embodies precisely what Israel has learned about the land: being without land makes it possible to trust the promise of it, while grasping land is the sure way to lose it. The powerful are called to dispossession. The powerless are called to power. The landed are called to homelessness. The landless are given a new home. (Brueggemann 2002:109)

Another participant noted how in order to know where you are leading, you need to know where you have come from. However, to be so caught up in the past is to jeopardize a vision for the future: '[the] scripture[s] of Israel and the church provide us with a powerful vision of home, a devastatingly truthful picture of home breaking, and an empowering hope for homecoming' (Bouma-Prediger and Walsh

2008:xii). Others reflected on the fact that all too often the destination of the Christian journey is constructed as heaven. However, 'too much heaven on the mind' fails to convey to people that Christianity is a truly life-enhancing experience now. Many felt that an over-emphasis on heaven could become a distraction from earth; moreover the importance of the Christian journey rather than an arrival at a destination was paramount. One had to ground the Kingdom in the present, immediate context. In imaging the final call for 'hands to the plough' one participant took out a cigarette packet. His father had been a farmer and he could remember his father putting a cigarette packet on the hedge at each end of the field. He kept his eye on this object so that his furrows would be straight. The mark is in the distance, but it allows effective and guided vision of the terrain in between. The participant noted that likewise you have to have a clear sense of God's mission within a place, and a clear reference point for that, otherwise you are likely to steer off course, or even worse look back from the plough (and risk losing limbs) rather than journey forward.

One of the key elements that emerged in the consciousness of the groups during interaction with this final biblical narrative was that a true 'sense of place' existed within relationships above localities. For ministerial practice this was particularly true, for clergy regularly move in and out of communities. While they can frequently become a point of reference for that locality (people know who they are) their vocation calls them again and again to move out of that place to another. In this movement it is the story of scripture that travels with them and their personal story that involves all the relationships they have made in the past. One participant summed this up well in her drawing of the command to 'go and follow' as taking a 'tabernacle' of place with her (God's and her story). This story, rather than anywhere she happened to stop at, was her true place.

Contextual Bible Study among clergy: a fresh expression of Church?

I opened this chapter by outlining recent developments in theological training, which is coming to be conceived more as formation of the whole Christian community than just a professional few. Joyce

Ann Mercer accordingly constructs her role as a seminary teacher as equipping her students with

> as many tools and as much confidence as possible so that they can interpret scripture in community and respond to God's call among us. Since our task is in communities of faith, part of our preparation includes taking into account the people participating in those communities. (2005:290)

Pritchard, in his recent book *The Life and Work of a Priest* (2007), similarly upholds the utility of collective reflection of those in ministry in order to allow them in turn to pursue collective reflection within the communities they seek to serve. First, he sees that through such collaborations one starts to see one's individual ministry as part of a community and partnership of 'ministers in mission' (2007:132). Second, he sees that collaborative work transforms one's perspective from 'guarding boundaries to growing relationships', not fearfully protecting territory as much as boldly promoting outside networks (2007:133). Third, he contends that groupwork allows one to start to think less about delegation and more about shared ministry (2007:134). Such collaboration rather than domination allows one not only to encourage ordained but also more importantly lay personnel within communities. Fourth, he sees collaboration as crucial if one is ever going to move beyond a 'self-preservation' outlook to one that embraces both growth and celebration (2007:136).

Contextual Bible Study likewise works from the principle that egalitarian dialogues around biblical texts can be constructed and in turn reform communities. This involves a certain challenge to those who are traditionally perceived as the 'expert' or 'professional'; it also provides a context in which those who have little confidence, or whose voice is infrequently heard, to participate. The challenge in initiating such contextual reflections among clergy was that each 'expert' needed to experience and enter into a more democratic process of interpretation, which they could then transplant to their own communities. The use of various media of art and performance to reflect theologically on conversations that people had experienced 'around' the biblical stories was not only an important part in displacing these clergy from their comfort zone (even their position of authority) but also in allowing them to experience vulnerability ('I can't paint, dance or be dramatic!'). The very honest contributions to the Contextual Bible Study dialogue about people's own perceived weaknesses, exhaustion and fear of failure (imaged in the lost son parable) were very moving in this respect. The process also offered the clergy an opportunity to explore less 'wordy' sides of their characters and imaginatively contemplate the biblical stories anew. Visual images are central in many modes of understanding, for 'our minds are more like art galleries than libraries' (Pritchard 2007:34). Edward Gibbs and Ryan Bolger point out in reference to this that since the Protestant Reformation an inordinate importance has been put on logic: 'linear progression of thought, highly reasoned exegesis and expository preaching' (Gibbs and Bolger 2006:20). They contend that oral, aural and visual models of interpretation could more readily appeal to people in postmodern contexts who thirst for 'meaningful activities' involving 'the convergence of sound, sight, and touch through activities, rituals and stories' (Gibbs and Bolger 2006:20). Akin to Contextual Bible Study's emphasis on multi-modal interpretations here 'the individual stories of each member and the collective story of the faith community are seen in the context of God's story as it unfolds through scripture . . . Theology becomes a dynamic, unfolding reflection of God's dealings with people in the changing circumstances of life' (Gibbs and Bolger 2006:164).

In many respects this sort of engaging sensory method has some crossovers with models of emerging church. Emerging church gatherings have first, as their central identity, an alignment with the life of Jesus in service and 'being with' people; the Contextual Bible Study model likewise is founded on a 'being with' and 'listening to' voices on the ground. Second, emerging church is suspicious of labelling realms as sacred or secular, they see all areas of life as potentially 'holy'; this was reiterated among the ministers' comments in the Contextual Bible Studies, regarding the possibilities of rethinking ancient church buildings and their uses to reach more people outside. Perhaps the profoundest image that questioned sacred/secular boundaries was the clergy imaging the Church in the 'travelling' community coming back from Passover; also the conception of 'place' as tabernacle, stories and relationships carried with you, rather than a specific location or site labelled as sacred. Third, emerging churches have a highly communal element whereby welcome and service to those outside the group is encouraged, and egalitarian participation within the group is central (Gibbs and Bolger 2006:45). The fact that the image of Jesus in the temple with the teachers of the law was emphasized as a 'dialogue' image was an important parallel here. Moreover, when clergy adopt the Contextual Bible Study method within lay contexts, they become just one voice among many. Fourth, with close reflection on context and the world 'outside' the Church, many emerging church movements have acknowledged a change of perspective as regards the story they are called to tell. One informant from an emerging church in California states: 'We got the gospel wrong: we were living in the wrong story. We were telling the story of modernity and Baby Boom aspirations rather than the radical message of the Kingdom' (Scandrette in Gibbs and Bolger 2006:49). The powerful question posed by one participant concerning what vision people had of the ship of the Church, 'Was it a lifeboat or merely a passenger ferry?', likewise seems to pose difficult but necessary questions about the Church and the story they are promoting. Finally, emerging churches conceive of the Church in open relationship, multiple circles of interaction within the wider community come into view in the reflection process: 'The practice of community formation is more central than the church meeting. Thus, an emerging church community seeks the Kingdom in all realms as it serves as a way of life for its people' (Gibbs and Bolger 2006:44). The various inputs from the clergy regarding co-operation with outside agencies and the realization that one should not just think of the Church in linear terms, in which one is 'locked into the internal problems of decline and ageing of the church membership', but rather spatially, which allows openness to 'the theological interpretation and practical renewal of the congregation as temple-like places of divine encounter for a diverse community of neighbours as well as members' (Cameron *et al.* 2005:185), seems another important resemblance between emerging church and Contextual Bible Studies.

The call to ministry is a costly one, it is also a great privilege: 'a life-changing vocation that is *lived out* and *lived into*' throughout one's whole life (Cocksworth and Brown 2006:223). Such individuals are trusted with leadership of worshipping communities and frequently perform central rites of passage for those in the wider culture. They are called to be one and at the same time insider and outsider, native and prophet, teacher and servant. Moreover, all ministries have to be earthed in local contexts and responsive to current cultural trends. Theirs is a leadership that is, like Christ's, radically collaborative, involving a 'being with' people. Perhaps given the vulnerability but also the humour that was displayed by many of the ministers in the artistic and performative sessions following the Contextual Bible Studies, the image of a conductor of an orchestra offered by Pritchard is a fitting one with which to end. It sums up the perils and possibilities, challenges and joys of collaborative endeavours which seek to empower and encourage others. He writes: 'We share the risks of the performance with the orchestras we serve. Any live performance has about it the adrenaline-rushing potential for greatness, mere adequacy or total disaster . . . Pray [to] the Great Composer for the best performance we can imagine' (Pritchard 2007:110).

Part III

THE WORD IN PLACE: PROSPECTS AND POSSIBILITIES

9

The hermeneutics of place

> The Bible is a significant text in the many struggles of our time...
> We are all trying to read the Bible other-wise.
>
> Gerald West

Leslie Houlden has given a less than enthusiastic response to 'contextual readings' of the sort outlined in Part II of this book, which he regards as 'little more than the discernment of scriptural analogies to present situations and concerns'. In his opinion 'the Bible has other jobs to do than dance to our late twentieth century tunes' (Houlden 1990, cited in Rowland 2006a:3). Christopher Rowland has forcefully rebutted this critique by reference to the critical importance of 'actualizing' (living and performing) scripture within contemporary communities. He realizes that these ancient texts produced in a context largely alien to our own are hard to translate into substance, but the pointers they give towards action are useful. In this way 'the words become the catalyst for discernment of the divine way in the present... They are not prescriptions, but intellectual and ethical stimuli, and means of encouragement' (Rowland 2006a:7). In reading 'with' others one is also challenged to recognize critically the power structures or ideologies by which one's own readings operate. Ched Myers has provocatively stated that 'throughout the ages this "people's book" keeps getting expropriated by the expert scribal classes. Jesus himself complained bitterly of this betrayal' (Myers 2006:33). By allowing stories to be contextualized in different worldviews, new perspectives are offered. Implicit within this model is the belief that to talk about the authority of scripture is to talk primarily about acceptance of the scripture, as a story that people can, to differing degrees, inhabit and live by. In Bob Ekblad's words, 'we need to leave Jerusalem and take our own journeys towards Emmaus opening ourselves to encounters with strangers' through which our eyes can see differently (Ekblad 2005:3). Philip Sheldrake, in his study of place, likewise recognized:

> It is only by enabling alternative stories to be heard that an 'elitist history' may be prised open to offer an entry point for the oppressed who have otherwise been excluded from the history of public places . . . Rather than abolish narrative we need to ask 'Whose narrative has been told?' 'Who belongs within the story of this place?'
>
> (Sheldrake 2001:19)

This book's central thesis has been that a recovery of a sense of place can in part be accomplished through Contextual Bible Studies: these promote the sharing of stories among a group, face-to-face interaction and the common and collective task of contextualizing scripture within particular 'places' (understood as shared location, vocation or experience). The process of Contextual Bible Study that encourages reflection and the sharing of stories is a powerful tool for 'place-making' for 'we need to know how elements of landscape play back into human processes of socialization and empowerment in spatial as well as temporal terms' (Bender 1992:741). Such 'story/narrative' pursuits have also been used as powerful tools to assemble new identities, strengthen relationships and uncover 'hidden transcripts' of communities and collectives. Charlotte Linde (2001), for example, in her study of narrative induction into organizations, sees the 'process of being encouraged or required to hear [and] understand' someone else's story alongside one's own as central in not only the forging of corporate identity but also mobilizing institutional reform.

Contextual Bible Study is not an abstract pursuit but rather one that draws attention to the particular and local through encounters, idioms, customs and memories. It urges groups to try and decipher dominant stories within communities and in response to the inspiration of biblical texts hear those that offer a different perspective in order to confront or question long-held assumptions. In this respect Contextual Bible Study is always critical, for by allowing different voices to rub up against one another the facilitator initiates dialogue and attunes members of the group to the unacknowledged gaps within their story-making and spotlights the cleavages that may exist between their presumed 'ideal' and their actual 'reality'. Such insights can then play a part in the envisioning of future transformation. In Joyce Ann Mercer's words, 'in the spirit of Marx's comment about philosophy . . . the goal is not simply to understand . . . but to be intentional about efforts to bring about change' (Mercer 2005:293). Contextual Bible Study could also be seen as a transformative ritual.

Jonathan Z. Smith famously characterized ritual as 'first and foremost a mode of paying attention . . . a process of marking interest' (1987:103). Context and place then are central components of ritualism, for these likewise direct attention to the local, the particular and the face to face. Akin to this, ritual theorists have time and again noted how rituals become important tools in the overcoming of conflict within communities. If some readings have been privileged over others then Contextual Bible Study from 'place' is an important corrective in rehabilitating those muted voices. The anthropological understanding of boundary-crossing rituals is often summed up in the symbolism of the body created, mutilated and reborn. It takes little imagination to plot the Contextual Bible Study dynamic onto this sort of ritualistic transformation. Individuals are brought together in the process, and in a democratic and open forum (some could say a liminal space) stories are shared and a new vision of community and place emerges. It is no accident that 'regeneration' jargon so often used in urban planning initiatives, as noted in Chapter 4, is itself a resurrection image. The perspectives gained on one's own story in reference to other participants' stories are clear: 'God calls people out of place so that their social and cultural experience can enhance the future meanings of communal faith' (Irizarry 2003:375).

The five groups that I have 'read with' in this book have provided a rich seam of multivocal responses to the biblical narratives encountered. Each group has offered some insight into 'dominant' and more resistant 'hidden' transcripts within their place. 'Reading in a city' echoed in parts the 'tourist' tales of Plymouth imaged in the great explorers of bygone ages and the glory days of the dock industries. However, at the same time, the wounded nature of the place that they inhabited (most notably imaged in the identification of Devonport with the place of pigs and dissolute living in the parable of the lost son) was also honestly shared. Urban degeneration, the influx of asylum-seekers, the sex trade and widespread drug and alcohol addiction were painful urban scars for the group. Overcoming the 'structural sins' identified were important parts in the construction of a new story in the regeneration plan for the area that marshalled 'faithful capital' within the community.

'Reading in a rural village' identified a strong commitment to the picture of a 'rural idyll' summed up in the theme of 'home'; so much so that this group did not seem to want to consider, in the first instance, the reality of evil or exclusion within their place. However, scratching beneath this initially positive surface, problems regarding rising house prices and the economic plight of farmers were honestly confronted and communicated within the group dialogues. Moreover, the cyclical nature of the seasons (considered in reference to 'foxes having holes and birds having nests, but the Son of Man having nowhere to lay his head') and the reality of death (and 'leaving the dead to bury the dead') within rural cultures provided food for thought as regards the necessity of change and development within their place.

'Reading in a fishing village' underscored the important role that the 'sea' as a metaphor of life played within this coastal community. The ambiguity of the sea as both life-giver and life-taker was a central trope in the stories shared. The perceived geographic and social marginality of Newlyn (not being part of the tourist trail and the fishing industry suffering debilitating pressures from government quotas etc.) also provided deep commentaries on the watery instability of their life and livelihoods. The regeneration of Trinity Methodist Chapel itself became symbolic of 'journeys across the lake to found a new people' and re-imagining of 'sanctuary' as a place of wider community participation than a worshipping congregation. This story of renewal was a constant inspiration for the group and in essence constituted a profound 'place-making' endeavour.

'Reading among the Deaf' was to engage with stories that disrupt and subvert the dominant 'hearing' transcript which labels this (sign-) language minority group as 'dis-abled'. The strong trend to recontextualize the biblical narratives within Deaf experience (deaf characters frequently being transplanted into biblical stories) was itself a compelling way of re-membering the text for a community that has so often been exiled from the dominant 'hearing' culture. Moreover, the powerful ways in which vision and performance were prized was itself a challenge to hearing culture's dominating medium of printed 'words'. This group, probably more than any others, most easily inscribed their lived experience into their performances of the biblical texts. They transformed a story of marginalization into a celebration of 'Deaf-way'.

'Reading among the clergy' was to engage with a 'professional' class in respect to scriptural interpretation. However, in the Contextual

Bible Study process they too were encouraged to participate as one among many in a collaborative and egalitarian group. The trials of ministry, including fatigue, the perilous positions of being both insider and outsider within a community and the dismal decline in church attendance were honestly dealt with. The picture of a pilgrim people imaged in the 'travelling community' coming back from Passover became evocative for their role in seeing 'place' as God's presence in one's story, rather than a physical locality. The representation of the Church as boat also provided fertile reflection on the nature of the ecclesiastical vessel in which they sailed. The clergy conferences themselves framed artistic reflections on the Contextual Bible Studies as part of the activities; this encouraged the ministers to experience vulnerability through trying out new things. Through this, their interdependence was highlighted and the ethos of 'emerging church', which encourages expressions of Christ in response to the realities of postmodern contexts, was experienced.

In short, all five groups witness that biblical texts find new meanings in encounters with different contexts: in this respect the biblical stories

> are like sojourners who hardly ever go back to the habitat they left behind. Texts in essence are moulded by the context in which they are located . . . it is not possible to finalize a text or restrict it to one context, or predetermine its meaning.   (Sugirtharajah 2003:576)

'Hermeneutics', the act of interpretation, witnesses to the contextuality of all understanding. To be able to comprehend and interpret, one needs to begin with particular interests and questions. No one interprets from nowhere; furthermore, texts do not have evident meaning without a reader. Texts do not in themselves speak, only interpreters do. Texts cannot live until someone responds and is stimulated by them in a particular place.

Readers themselves may inhabit a number of different identities or places at once and Contextual Bible Studies cannot be innocent of the fact that group members can still choose which stories they will voice and share with others and which they will conceal. However, it is also true that 'canonized' or 'dominant' stories (often constructed from outside the place, or from the 'top down') were confronted with 'counter' or 'marginal' stories in each group's interpretation. This is a salutary rejoinder to all those critics who claim that the perils of eisegesis (a reading 'into' the text) or more boldly a 'prostitution of the text' haunt all contextual endeavours. In Fernando Segovia's words, such a criticism is meaningless, 'for in cultural studies *all exegesis is ultimately eisegesis*: interpretation and hermeneutics go hand in hand' (my italics, Segovia 1995:16). A perspective which encourages the readings of a number of contexts inhabited by members, to be brought together for reflection, also plays against the charge that such readings are solipsistic and isolationist. While a city's concerns may be very different to fishing villages, nonetheless wisdom regarding place-making can be re-imagined in each context. Moreover, read collectively these contextual interpretations provide a powerful dialogue with each other, for as Brian Blount contends,

> the full spectrum of meaning available in a text can only be appreci-ated by *allowing a multitude of communal interpretations to engage each other* . . . a text can be envisioned as a rainbow of potential meaning whose individual colours, while visible to one interpreter or commun-ity, are invisible to many others. (my italics, Blount 1995:178)

In fact it is only in the collision of various contextual readings that liberating narratives have been constructed: master narratives couched in patriarchy, slavery and racism have been exposed as oppressive by those counter stories from below. Perhaps this was not so much playing the 'violins' of oppression, but rather urging the powers that be to take up a new score of contrapuntal music that challenges the dominant beat. In the words of Richard Bauckham, 'Scripture may speak freshly to a lone individual or a marginal group in a way that challenges tradition and community and in a way that the church is initially unwilling to hear. We must allow for the Jeremiahs and Luthers' (Bauckham 2002:75).

Throughout all the groups' engagement with the four biblical stories I have come to appreciate how scriptural narratives are not just places to be inhabited by readers, but also point beyond themselves to the construction of stories yet untold. The various genres of the four biblical stories (parable, narrative, miracle, sayings) produced very different responses. The parable seemed to be most easily allegorized within the communities, whereas the sayings produced more loose connections with a context and more often than not focused on a particular image (the child, dead burying dead, lilies of the fields) to start to build connections. The christological images in the stories (Jesus as parable-teller, Jesus as boy, Jesus as miracle-worker, Jesus as sage) also encouraged different identifications. The readers were more often willing to identify with teachings of Jesus than contextualize themselves in his character. Only the clergy aligned the authority of Jesus with their own place of authority; other groups seemed more willing to engage with the picture of the child Jesus, but disinclined to identify with him as a miracle-worker. Similarly, the ways in which particular texts were more evocative in one community than another was also instructive. The fact that the farming community found more ready resonance in the parable of the lost son, and the fishing community were able to visualize the stilling of the storm narrative within their experience, is perhaps unsurprising. The fact, however, that Legion, localized as a fragmented and wounded place, spoke volumes in the inner-city redevelopment area, but seemed to have been harder to picture among the rural village and clergy, is an interesting touchstone for further reflection. Could it be, in line with Contextual Bible Studies' heritage, that certain contexts (particularly those marked by marginalization and oppression) are in the first instance more alive to the politically subversive nature of Jesus' mission than those communities that inhabit more 'centrist' positions in terms of social status and authority? Whatever one's conclusions, it is nevertheless true that, based on the results of this particular study, it seems that place is an analogical notion, and it is understood in different ways in different places and differently in response to different texts.

It is also true that the artistic and performative endeavours witnessed in the fishing village's map-making, the clergy's artistic workshops and the Deaf group's visualizing of the text in British Sign Language also offered suggestive ways of contextualizing the text anew. Artistic pursuits were important means by which one could explore the possibilities of texts, beyond purely logo-centric interpretations. As many subaltern interpretative methods (including performance, using the text as a ritual object etc.) have taught us, one can be assaulted into alternative ways of discerning the 'word in place' through various artistic means. In a similar vein, Kari Latvus has recently submitted that the use of 'bibliodrama', a method inspired by both socio- and psychodrama, which utilizes role play in the identification of particular biblical characters and situations, may likewise provide an important key for folk interpretations to envisage not only exegesis but more importantly 'socially orientated Bible reading' (Latvus 2007:139).

Trying to pull some of these disparate thoughts together, the ways in which the respective groups contextualized the narratives can offer us some pointers for understanding the 'hermeneutics' operative in the groups' perceptions of the 'word in place'. I contend that three main strategies of interpretation marked various group responses: allegory, parable and midrash.

Allegory

Allegory has been a reading strategy of interpreters of Christian scripture since the patristic era. Donald McKim defines allegory as 'saying something different from what one reads in a written source' with the direct aim of 'allowing a legitimate interpretation of the cultural tradition' (McKim 1998:6). A text could speak via particular mappings of elements of a biblical story to a contemporary historical/cultural context. As a result the reader would become 'privy to what otherwise [could not] be discerned in the text' (Yarchin 2004:xiv). Origen of Alexandria believed that literal interpretations would produce readings undeserving of God, a mere 'bodily' sense. One needed to delve into the text's 'soul' through allegory in order to appreciate how every entity and experience is in fact a pointer to a more profound spiritual truth:

> Just as the visible and invisible, earth and heaven, soul and flesh, body and spirit have mutually this kinship and this world is a result of their union, so also we must believe that Holy Scripture results from the visible and the invisible.　　(Origen, *Homilies on Leviticus* 5:1)

Origen's anthropology accordingly pictured human beings as created in the image of God, tooled with the ability to discern and respond to scripture's message. Building on Origen's legacy many others throughout the Christian centuries have produced biblical interpretations to speak directly to the contexts and challenges of their own eras and situations. However, with the rise of rationalist and Enlightenment-informed historical criticism, such 'pre-modern' pursuits were largely lost. It is perhaps no accident that, in the rise of advocacy and subaltern approaches such as Dalit and liberation models outlined above in Chapter 2, an allegorical plotting of the interpreter's experience onto the text has once again been explicitly pursued. Indeed any 'contextualizing' endeavour that needs to take text, interpreter's context and a commitment to action within the world seems dependent on having some allegorical dimensions. The text that was most easily allegorized by the groups I worked with was perhaps unsurprisingly the parable of the lost son. All groups plotted either a character or a place directly from the story into their own context. Devonport was imaged in the 'far-off country'; the farmer in Drewsteignton was seen in the elder son; the lost son's re-evaluation of home was evidenced in the Trinity Chapel's re-evaluation of worship space achieved in their time in the Seamen's Mission; various biblical characters interchangeably became Deaf in the interpretations of the Deaf group; the Church became the father's welcome in the artistic conceptions of the priests. Another 'image' that was easily allegorized by the fishing village, the city and the priests, was the boat as the Church in the stilling of the storm narrative. Yet the questions asked of the boat – Whom does she belong to? What type of boat is she? – point far beyond a straight allegorical interpretation to something more creative.

Parable

Parable as a genre casts one concept alongside another, in order to encourage new understandings to emerge. Parables invite interpreters to 'discern the word' in different times, places and situations. Moreover, their currency is, as Jesus' own parable-telling reveals, couched in the commonplace ('they are not about "giants of the faith" who have religious visions', McFague 1974:630), even if at the same time they assault expectations of the 'normal'. Paul Ricoeur saw that parabolic or metaphorical thinking could throw together previously distinct entities in order to push meaning beyond the known and provide a 'new dimension of reality and truth' (Ricoeur 1995:10). In essence the parabolic conjures up alternative visions. In Rowan Williams's words, 'it displays a possible world, a reality in which any human reality can find itself, and in inviting me into its world the text breaks open and extends my possibilities' (Williams 2000, cited in Graham, Walton and Ward 2005:65).

In the interpretations offered in the groups I worked with, a number of instances of a metaphor 'used in an unfamiliar context to give new insight' moving groups 'to see the ordinary world in an extraordinary way' (McFague 1974:632) were given. In these parabolic understandings the biblical stories were seen less as transparent windows that could simply be looked through to neatly plot the biblical story in another context and more like intricate works of art, which needed to be pondered and contemplated. The way in which the temple was contrasted with the travelling group in the readings of the priests led for example to a new conception of 'God's presence' and 'story' as 'tabernacle' carried with them in ministry. Similarly, in relation to the image of 'leaving the dead to bury the dead' the Devonport readers told stories about the rebirth of their cemetery as a community space. To give another example, the youth dance in Newlyn that encouraged the choreography of the youngest member, and their street dancing in various parts of the village to emphasize their perceived 'displacement' in reference to the image of the 'Son of Man having nowhere to lay his head', also juxtaposed scripture and context to offer new illumination. Sallie McFague notes that an interpretation rooted in the parabolic often employs autobiography or more creative avenues of expression, for these genres more readily 'manifest the ways metaphor operates in language, belief and life' (McFague 1974:631). In short, unlike allegory, this mode of interpretation does not just supplant one image for another but rather 'reformulates' and 'recontextualizes' to offer new and transforming visions.

Midrash

Daniel Boyarin, in his essay 'Placing Reading' (1993), contrasts the oral and public performance of ancient Jewish Torah reading with the privatized cathartic reading of medieval European and Christian cultures. The fact that within Contextual Bible Study the text is orally performed before others is accordingly a step towards a more communal engagement with it.

Midrash, derived from the Hebrew meaning 'to search out', constitutes a mode of Jewish interpretation that attempts to fill in gaps and pose questions between the scriptural text and contemporary culture (Sherwood 2000:100). The group I worked with that seemed to exhibit 'midrashic' interpretation most explicitly was the Deaf group. The myriad readings of the parable of the lost son and the very strong emphasis on weaving Deaf culture into the fabric of both this parable and the other biblical narratives encountered (including the retelling of the crossing of the lake story in BSL), corroborates the association with midrash which Daniel Boyarin has recently identified as involving 'interpreting and completing the text in accordance with the codes of [the midrashist's] culture' (Boyarin 1990:14). Midrash explicitly explains the contemporary relevance of scripture and retells scriptural stories to impart immediacy of the story within the living community. Accordingly midrash is not to be understood as 'a noun but a verb, a function and activity' (Rotenberg 1986:42). Mordechai Rotenberg suggests that midrash guarded Jewish survival through its techniques of self-renewal that alleviated cognitive dissonance between present reality and past experience. It enabled 'each generation to relive anew such root experiences as the Exodus from Egypt and its miraculous revelation of God' (Rotenberg 1986:43). The past is retold for the present life of the community. In essence midrash is rehabilitative story-telling that stretches, realigns and shapes a malleable text into contemporary relevance. The results may have been very different if the texts used within this study were those in which metaphors of sensory impairment played a more prominent role (for instance in the 'social association of disability and moral laxity', Melcher 2007:129). Perhaps the group would not so easily have translated their Deaf experience and culture into the fabric of 'texts of Deaf terror', or maybe in contrast they would have subversively constructed resistant midrashim which ideologically 'took sacred elements of rabbinic thought and then inverted them against their sacred origins' (Handelman 1982, cited in Sherwood 2000:100); one thing is certain, more contextual readings of this sort undoubtedly need to be pursued.

My role as facilitator and ethnographer

The Russian literary critic Mikhail Bakhtin famously identified engagement as central to mobilizing a community. For him true dialogues could only become real in understanding and response (Bakhtin 1981:281). One voice that perhaps needs contextualizing in the dialogues presented thus far is mine, as both facilitator of the groups and an ethnographer (a person who has written up the field-work in a particular manner). Academic narratives about community exchanges, even those that have self-consciously read alongside and recorded voices rather than participating directly in the conversations, document these in a particular framework for consumption by others. Folk voices in 'transcription' can lose some of their particularity, reflexivity and contradictory tensions (although I have tried hard to record these as directly as possible). Moreover, I am not blind to the fact that recording exchanges on paper means 'voices [are] mediated and used by academics for particular purposes' (Riley and Harvey 2005:272), in this instance for constructing pointers to rehabilitate a sense of place. I was very aware as I wrote up my field-work how I caught myself more positively responding to particular 'marginal' interpretations (particularly the Deaf group and those from the inner city) and was more critical of those from more 'centrist' positions recorded by the group from the rural village and the clergy conferences. As a result I must openly acknowledge that I may well have coloured my accounts of the fieldwork at certain points with elements of suspicion and correction. These colourings I suspect emerged from how far I perceived the respective groups to be, in line with the aims of the Contextual Bible Study movement, offering a platform for silenced voices from the borders of life. The records presented in this book should therefore be recognized as yet another contextual 'story-telling' endeavour, for all ethnography is in essence narrative. However, Jonathan Boyarin defends the ethnographic perspective in his belief that all tradition engages in a constant process of reverbalization and reinscription. Thus not only the collective responses to the texts recorded in Part II, but also the ethnographic frameworks I have presented these results within, 'should be able to become part of that process' of dialogue (Boyarin 1989:415). Each community will be encouraged to read my analysis and respond to it, this is the messy business of discerning the word in place: 'to start with the ordinary and the everyday, with personal life, with corporate stories, with "our times" in their political and social agony, is [likewise] the bold business of theology' (McFague 1974:645).

I have submitted that the 'hermeneutics of place' as exhibited in Contextual Bible Studies here seem to cluster around allegorical, parabolic and midrashic modes of interpretation. These modes of interpretation are of course nothing new, they have been practised from the earliest times as profound means by which people have been encouraged to make not only fresh meanings based on scripture, but also build agendas to embody scripture in their own particular times and situations. Contextual Bible Study, in this respect, is no new endeavour, but rather a 're-membering', a 're-traditionalizing', of well-worn Christian interpretative methods that had for a time, in the post-Enlightenment period, been side-stepped. Yet the utility of these models of understanding, for liberating the personal and collective stories of readers from the straitjacket of dispassionate 'modernist' modes of interpretation, surely has a part to play in rescuing biblical studies from 'the boredom of conventional and impersonal reading of the Bible, from separating a person from the scholar, from suppression of innermost desire of what a critic wants to say' (Moore 1995, cited in Nelavala 2006:65). They likewise have a part to play in true discernment of the word in various contexts, a word that itself was most profoundly imaged 'in place' by 'pitching his tent among us' (John 1.14).

10

'Being hefted in scripture': the spirit of Christian place-making

[Scripture's] story has transforming power only as it intersects with our individual life stories and the broader collective history in which we live.

John Vincent

A recently published article in *The Times* asked 'Are you Hefted?' (Macintyre 2007). Totally ignorant of what 'hefted' meant, let alone whether I could be described as such, I read on with interest. It turns out the word 'hefted' is used of sheep that have inherited from their forebears a profound sense of place, an inbred, inbuilt and intimate knowledge of their land. So much so that hefted flocks can be left to roam free with no restrictions, instinctively know where therapeutic plants can be found and, according to wind direction, will identify where shelter is most likely. A hefted flock would never voluntarily leave their land, for to do so would be quite literally to forget who they were. This was underlined a few years ago in the physical moving of hefted flocks in the foot and mouth crisis. Many herds were destroyed and others so disorientated that electric fencing needed to be erected on their return. In losing their land they lost their memory and their sense of self and as a result of their displacement had to completely re-envisage their own identity.

In Chapter 1 I documented the industrialized Western world's promotion of what anthropologists have defined as 'non-places': husks bereft of face-to-face embodied interaction and common stories. Such non-places promote both physical and ideological displacement: disengagement of individuals from their immediate locality and community. Such dynamics contribute to the erosion of any sense of 'heftedness' within many contemporary contexts, including rural ones. For while a 'hefted' psychology may still be apparent in some close-knit rural villages, even there, as has been witnessed in Chapter 5, an emergence of second-home culture, rising house prices and the lack of opportunities for the young have had a real effect on the capabilities and shape of collectives as authentic 'places'. Steven Croft, reflecting theologically on such developments, urges Christians not to see these cultural dynamics as deadly and insurmountable threats, but rather to take seriously the realities of the contexts in which they operate. He writes:

> I see a Church that is beset by anxiety about the future . . . fed by an almost continual blizzard of prophecies of doom and decline. We need to make wise decisions in order to shape our future . . . our decisions need to be guided, tested and shaped by scripture. In a storm the boat needs its keel perhaps more than its rudder. *Our decisions also need to be informed by the realities of the world in which we find ourselves.*
> (my italics, 2006:viii)

Croft's main insight is that there is a real and urgent need for reconceiving a Christian 'place-making' agenda in reference to the specific contextual needs and circumstances of contemporary human communities.

In responding to Croft's insight, this book has submitted that Christians are at base a storied people, called to live out 'good news' within their day-to-day lives and allowing that story to identify, expose and challenge those alternative cultural stories that do not promote authentic manifestations of 'place' within their contexts. In John Riches and Susan Miller's terms,

> a close, critical reading of the Bible can provide the context in which participants can articulate views contrary to and subversive of the official discourse of Church (and society) which may inhibit and control them in ways of which they are barely conscious. (2006:123)

This challenge continues at a practical level, for in living into the story of scripture, one is engaged by it, in Ched Myers' terms, as a 'spec-actor': one who is 'open to allowing the story to challenge their own life-scripts' and ultimately 'to let the story read them' (Myers *et al.* 1996:xi).

In this sense the spirit of a Christian place-making agenda must primarily be one that identifies how the story of scripture challenges one to facilitate transformation in one's own context. As Part II of this book has shown, the issues on the ground for a rural village, inner city, fishing village, the Deaf and clergy are very different. Similarly, while the same biblical stories were encountered by each group, the wisdom drawn from these texts in the respective contexts was also very different. Thus, a recovery of a sense of place is facilitated through discerning the wisdom of scripture in *specific* and *particular* contexts. In this respect Christian place-making endeavours must be rooted and formed in disciplines akin to 'cross-cultural training', for if Christian place-making endeavours misread the immediate contexts in which they seek to effect change, their actions will amount to nothing.

Michael Langrish (Bishop of Exeter) has likewise petitioned the Church to 'read the cultural contexts' in which it seeks to be a true and authentic expression of community. In his opinion, the Church should be both contributive to, and exemplary of, a place ideal. He has constructed eight very helpful principles to demonstrate the Church's calling to link into all systems of human society and model true community in its various contexts (Langrish 2004:36–8). It is also an agenda that has profound parallels with the Contextual Bible Study approach. First, Langrish urges the Church to be 'incarnational' and embodied: physically involved in, attending to, and 'being with' the immediate community. The 'hermeneutics of presence' central to the Contextual Bible Study method is of course at one with this aim. Second, he urges the Church to be a 'unifying' force, ever exposing and critiquing exclusionary maps of meaning and itself creating a truly inclusive community in every context in which it is present (work, education, leisure etc.). The means by which participants in this book were encouraged to consider those 'out of place' according to their respective dominant maps of meaning is an example of this. Third, he urges the Church to be 'fuzzy edged' and 'open-doored', offering free and welcome access to all people and never giving the appearance of being a private members' association. Although it is often hard to orchestrate, the fruitful dialogues that can be initiated through the Contextual Bible Study method with those considered outsiders to church communities can be instructive. The rural village group in this project, for example, consisted of both church attendees and non-attendees. The exchanges between these individuals throughout the process brought greater mutual understanding. Fourth, Langrish implores the Church to be 'celebratory', involved in 'marking interest' (providing rituals and hosting traditions) in local community life and performing rites of passage for the people. Contextual Bible Study could in itself also be conceived, as outlined in the previous chapter, as a ritual of status transformation, by which communities are brought together to share, remember and reinstitute important events and memories in the life of their community. Fifth, he envisions the Church as a community to be 'light on structures': everyone's talents should be sought out and used, and there should be no feeling of enforced hierarchies or glass ceilings preventing full involvement and participation. This is one of the central tenets of the Contextual Bible Study movement, namely that voices previously muted or excluded are given a forum for expression. It is a democratic and participatory method. Sixth, Langrish cautions that 'buildings', while being taken seriously, must never become ends in themselves. Questions like 'Who is this building for?' and 'What other activities and sectors of the society could it host?' need to be candidly asked. The redevelopment of Trinity Methodist Chapel in Newlyn as a community space for artistic, performative and community groups seems a particularly potent symbol of this sort of re-imagination of space. Seventh, he believes the Church as model community should have a 'culture of nurture and growth' whereby corporate interdependence as well as individual gifts can be nourished. Contextual Bible Study accordingly promotes community exchanges and dialogues that encourage people to conceive of their place as a nexus of values, experiences and shared visions. My 'Reading in a city' illustrated just this. The participants started to understand their city as a living being that could be wounded and abused, but also, through the mobilization of social capital, healed and made whole. Finally, and most importantly, Langrish submits that the Church 'should have a spiritually growing people' who are themselves 'hefted' in scripture and who exhibit the reality of God's love in all contexts in which they operate. In this manner, as Langrish concludes, the Church will be enabled as

catalyst, facilitator, learner, participant, advocate and prophet of true community at every level of community with which it is involved . . . The Church in its work of community needs to engage, and be equipped to engage, in a variety of different forums . . . to be faithful to its calling and effective in its mission task.

(Langrish 2004:40)

In Langrish's scheme the Church is firmly rooted in the particular and local, embodying the scriptural story in specific contexts. His agenda also urges 'place-making' Christians to overcome false boundaries between a worshipping community and the wider community. This insight shares some links with the vision of the 'emerging church movement' (referred to in Chapter 8), which also seeks to overcome sacred/secular divides in the project of the sacralization of all contemporary cultures and communities and the creative enmeshing of the Kingdom within all civilization.

If these dimensions are all parts of a dynamic place-making agenda, I want to end by mentioning three additional dimensions that have not been featured at all, hitherto, within this book. My focus has been firmly on embodied, human communities and relationships but the following themes also offer important touchstones for theological reflection on the notion of authentic 'place': the ecclesiastical parish; the internet; and ecology.

The ecclesiastical parish

If we are not 'hefted' in the way that communities, even a couple of generations ago were, then neither are we hefted in the way that the parish system originally envisaged. This model depended on the collective story of a community and their locality. The parish church provided a key focus for the residents and marked important personal and social occasions: it baptized children and was the place for the living to celebrate the community's departed. Graveyards surrounding the church were visible inscriptions of the circle of relationships both past and present, and a reminder of the inevitable circle of life and death. It is not without good reason that graveyards have accordingly been referred to as 'the open books' of the community; yet increasingly cemeteries are now situated on the outskirts of a town (Percy 2006:3–15). In this respect is it any accident that etymologically the word 'cemetery' does not even denote death but rather a 'dormitory' or 'sleeping place'? (Francis *et al.* 2005:xvii). Could this be further evidence of a move away from 'placing' the dead among the living, and a move towards a trend, symptomatic of the Western world's anaesthetizing to the realities of corporeal existence and its dissolution, a 'placing apart' of elements held to 'hold [a] powerful and disturbing charge that is not comfortably resisted' (Francis

et al. 2005:215). In a related vein, while church space was often perceived as community space used as a venue for debates, celebrations,
get-togethers – constituting a 'community comfort zone' in all its
senses – for many outside, it is now perceived as the exclusive space
of the worshipping community (Percy 2006:3–15). In my 'Reading
in a rural village' it was no coincidence that the 'place' the community said they would give up everything to retain was the local shop,
not the parish church. The shop was where personal exchanges took
place and neighbourly concern was demonstrated on a day-to-day
level. In light of this one can only admire the wisdom and foresight
of St Peter's Church, West Buckland, which situated the post office
within the church building, thus physically erasing a division between church and the local community. Similarly in my 'Reading in
a fishing village' the conversion of the Methodist chapel to a community space used by a variety of peoples for different cultural activities was seen by participants to encompass the idea of 'sanctuary' far
better than when the chapel was used exclusively by the worshipping
church. In short, a Christian 'place-making agenda' needs to reconsider the ways in which strengths of ecclesiastical parishes, particularly their potential links with the community wider than the church
alone, can be re-appropriated in an era of increasing 'dislocation'.

The internet: \<www.nonplacechurch.com\>

What impact, if any, have technological advances had on a Christian
place-making agenda? The so-called 'virtual church' is for many an
oxymoron, for since earliest times the Christian *ekklesia* has been
incarnated in interdependent communities focused on participation
in ritual, worship and the visible living out of the gospel. However,
it is also true that for those who do not have the time or the physical ability to attend church, then this could offer a potentially pro-
ductive alternative. I was very struck by one respondent at a clergy
training day I was leading, who fiercely rejected Marc Augé's cate-
gorization of cyberspace as 'non-place'. She recounted how after she
had converted to Christianity she had a number of questions she
wanted to ask but did not feel comfortable asking her fellow attendees or the priest; she therefore went to an online chat room and began
conversations there. But perhaps this in itself illustrates Augé's point:
the woman did not have to experience the vulnerability of embodied

interaction on the internet that she would have had to in 'real' life. Perhaps the greater lesson to be learnt is that boundaries of the Church need to appear 'lighter on structures' (to echo Langrish's phraseology) so people feel safe and welcome in an arena to ask difficult questions. Is it any wonder that so often the litmus test of online relationships is when one finally meets one's technological interlocutor 'in the flesh'? In a related vein it is perhaps no coincidence that in a recent edited volume on fresh expressions of church and emerging churches no examples of online churches are featured at all, in spite of the fact that the editors submit that 'post-modern people construct their world in nontextual and non-linear ways, and the gospel must be embodied and therefore communicated in that same manner to be faithful in mission' (Gibbs and Bolger 2006:70). While an essence of 'community' may not depend on face-to-face relationships, in light of this evidence I suspect that the essence of the Church as 'the body of Christ' still very much does. Continuing this theme, Lily Kong in her study of religion and technology ponders what role, if any, ritual can play in a technological sphere: 'how is social solidarity affected and what is the role of place in any new ritual practice? What role will rituals performed via technological means have vis-à-vis face-to-face communal rituals?' (Kong 2001:409) One can ask with her whether cyber-ritual practised in front of a computer screen can ever be an authentic replacement for embodied ritual, or like cyber-sex is it destined only ever to be a strange 'fantasy' which in the end falls short of the 'real' thing?

Of the contexts in which I worked, the Deaf community was perhaps the one that stood most to benefit from digital and technological advancements. Yet even here one participant saw the availability of the Bible in BSL on iPods and the use of webcams for sign language exchanges as both promise and peril, mainly because only a fortunate few were able to gain access to such technology (her friend in the developing world would not be able to enjoy a similar privilege). Likewise those housebound elderly who stand to most benefit from 'virtual' churches also may lack the requisite skills to operate technologies, for such know-how is more readily found within the younger generation.

Thus while many church communities now have web presences hoping to attract even one individual of the countless millions that walk through www.world every day, their main aim is still to bring these individuals to attend an embodied gathering. There is, it seems, room for much more reflection on the 'place' of online interaction and the rapidly transforming cyberscape within the Christian place-making project. My initial hunch would still be that place-making endeavours are more abundantly encountered in 'real' embodied humanity than 'virtual' information technologies.

Ecology

In its exclusive focus on human communities, this book has not attempted to elaborate on the ecology of place, yet this dimension also warrants consideration in a Christian place-making agenda. Adam, the primal human, is described as being formed from the matter of the earth and enlivened by the breath of God constituted in the planetary elements of wind and water. The human is an earth creature, but alone among such creatures, it has belligerently despoiled its own habitat. Its behaviour has fallen far short of the biblical ideal of stewardship. Grim yields of global warming, ecological degradation, pollution and biodiversity loss, and so on, are the stinking fruits of that wanton abuse and neglect. When humanity has viewed the earth as mere surroundings, it becomes negligible and disposable 'background'. Thus any way in which one can rekindle shared community with the earth should be an important constituent of a Christian place-making vision. Disregard of creation is symptomatic of a more serious plight of 'dislocation' that will eventually render humanity as not only ideologically, but also more irreversibly 'ecologically', homeless (Bouma-Prediger and Walsh 2008:158). Of course being hefted in scripture is to be hefted in a story that can disturb and challenge alternative cultural myths or 'other gospels' which preach toxic praxis. Timothy Gorringe claims that 'the free market' is itself a 'gospel which defines human progress in terms of consumption and which is driving the ecological crisis' (Gorringe 2006:27). In order to cultivate with integrity an abundant relationship with creation, one has to start to engage with the perspective of the earth and develop, on the strength of scripture's alternative voices, virtues that re-inscribe the interconnectedness of humanity with the rest of creation. In encouraging contextual reflections on the earth and non-human life, one is enabled to give these elements a voice. Tamsin Kerr (2006) has posited the 'land' as the original 'subaltern', for 'its interests can only be voiced by its colonisers [humanity]'. Various ecotheology projects that have sought to listen to the voice of the earth therefore have an important role to play here in resisting humanity's abusive power. Joanna Macy's concept of 'a parliament of all beings' in her book *Thinking Like a Mountain* (1993) and the ecojustice principles of the *Earth Bible Project* – 'intrinsic worth', 'interconnectedness', 'voice', 'purpose', 'mutual custodianship' and 'resistance' (Habel 2000:24) – attempt to discern both the character and cries of creation within the scriptural witness. In the constructions of Contextual Bible Studies why not try and discern the voice and personality of non-human elements (rivers, animals, trees etc.) encountered within scriptural texts and question how these can be liberated from human oppression?

'Being hefted in scripture': some conclusions

Anneliese Worster and Eleanor Abrams contend that a true 'sense of place' involves social knowledge which facilitates a developed social identity, attachments to both human and non-human communities and ecological knowledge (Worster and Abrams 2005:526). In many ways their pointers are akin to those that have been outlined here. Moreover, the agenda outlined above undoubtedly necessitates Christians to re-imagine their place within their own contexts in order to 'communicate afresh the good news to a new world' (Gibbs and Bolger 2006:19). If these cultural realities are not taken seriously the Church risks becoming 'the ecclesiastical equivalent of gated communities' (*Faithful Cities*, 2006:84), isolated and introverted.

I have submitted that Christian formation needs to take something akin to 'cross-cultural' training seriously to tool and enable people to 'discern the word' in different contexts to render in contextually appropriate forms 'the poiesis and the praxis, the truth and the justice, of God' (Vanhoozer 2002, cited in Ramachandra 2008:261). In response to this, the South West Ministry Training Course, and other formation schemes like it, place students in different contextual environments in order to develop their sensitivities to reflect theologically on place and to encourage them critically to evaluate stories for good and ill that students may hold. The Contextual Bible Study method outlined in this book is one means by which students are enabled to allow scripture to speak within, and challenge, present-

day contexts. In theologically 'forming' students in this way, programmes of contextual enquiry have some resonance with recent
developments in the medical curriculum, which now likewise often
focuses on people-centred, 'problem-based learning' (as opposed
to an exclusive focus on physiology) to practically equip students
with tools to face the realities and demands of a busy health-care
environment.

From its earliest conception, Christianity was a movement that
wished to embrace and reach out from the 'particular' to the whole
inhabited earth. In considering local manifestations of scripture and
theology, Vinoth Ramachandra has suggested that 'we can test the
local expressions of Christian faith against one another, thus mani-
festing the true catholicity of the body of Christ' (Ramachandra
2008:259). Likewise he cautions against any one local expression
being rendered normatively universal, even though its relevance
may be far ranging, for 'all Christian theologies endeavour to speak
truthfully (*albeit in broken speech*) of the universal God' (my italics,
Ramachandra 2008:259).

Being formed or 'hefted' in scripture is of course also to be formed
in a story that is still awaiting its conclusion. The contextualizing project is therefore part of an ongoing redemptive agenda for Christian
'place-making'. However, that scriptural story in itself always needs
to be the place where reflection begins, for ultimately we 'are not at
liberty to . . . act as if the place starts with us. If we change the story
line, import scenes from other plays or rewrite the ending, we have
another play and not the Christian one' (Ramachandra 2008:260).
While the contextual readings offered in this book all offer different
cultural and biographical reflections, they nonetheless all demonstrate
a commitment to construct wisdom that coheres with the Christian
story of salvation.

I opened this book by recalling the tragic chronicle of Hallsands,
a village that was swept into the sea on account of human abuse of
the natural environment and the muting of the resistant voices of the
villagers by those in power. In many ways this event offers a 'parable'
to a church that needs to listen and participate in local expressions
of community. The Church likewise, if it is to avoid becoming deso-
late cliff-top ruins, needs to seriously reconsider the natural habitats,
contexts and human realities in which it operates. While the Church
can at times seem to stand vulnerably and precariously on the edge

of threatening cultural tides, ironically it is often from these vantage points that new horizons can be encountered, new visions of future destinations gained and perhaps most importantly transformed visions of our present 'home' offered. It is this 'return' or 'homecoming' that is perhaps the most important 'Christian place-making' reflection of all. For it constitutes the 'radical' homecoming call of the shepherd who, in scripture, leaves behind the 99 (hefted?) sheep, in order to seek out the single one that was displaced.

Further resources for Contextual Bible Studies on place

As I mentioned in Chapter 3, ideally it would have been wonderful to work through an entire biblical text with the groups. Perhaps this is something you could pursue within your own respective contexts. The basic methodology is in essence quite simple. You need to read a section of the biblical text with the group, ask for immediate reactions, then tease out a theme or situation within the biblical text and encourage the group to form links between these and their own situations and contexts. In planning for the sessions, you may want to consider the format in which you will initially deliver the Bible narratives to the group. In my work I removed all chapter and verse notations so the text could be read more freely as a story. The version of the Bible used may also need consideration: for instance, a contemporary translation, such as *The Message*, may well aid group participants who have grown accustomed to certain versions to contextualize stories in their contemporary situations more easily. It may also work well as a more accessible text if the group includes non-Christians. That said, in my research I used the New Revised Standard Version (which uses inclusive language) so as not to offend participants on gender grounds. As with my work with the Deaf group, if the group you are working with has variable literacy levels you may want to consider presenting the text in visual or dramatic modes as an alternative to purely textual ones.

After you have introduced the text to the group, you will then need to probe both the biblical narrative and the contexts in which they are being read a little deeper and start to encourage the stories (biblical and contemporary) to dialogue with one another. The facilitator of the group may like to consult traditional commentaries in preparation for the Contextual Bible Study, for some members of the group may require clarification on aspects of the world 'behind the text' in order to let that speak more clearly to their present situations.

The facilitator also needs to encourage diverse viewpoints to engage with one another. In essence this is the only control that Contextual Bible Study methodology has against allowing a text to be uncritically read or received. If group members are initially reluctant to voice alternative opinions (or indeed if the group seems unanimous in its reading – which is highly unlikely given the diversity of individual experiences) then the facilitator may well want to encourage the group by voicing an alternative perspective and encouraging them to engage with this view. From the origins of the Contextual Bible Study method, strong trust has been put in the process to overcome conflict, allow a diversity of opinions to jostle alongside one another and, even if resolution is not found, guard against the threat of any one perspective becoming smugly complacent and dominant. For true transformation and self-critical analysis of a context to be achieved all members need to be open to new visions that may well assault convictions that were once uncritically assumed.

The Contextual Bible Study movement always urged groups to end the process with praxis: the gospel stories were to inspire action and renewal in the contemporary world. The facilitator of each group could accordingly sum up the main points of discussion raised within the session and encourage the group collectively to produce an action plan based on their deliberations that can be realistically accomplished within the wider community.

Another important part of the facilitation process is the use of various activities to encourage the groups to work together (as seen in the sample activities featured in Chapter 3). The nature of the activities adopted will of course largely depend on the settings in which one works. Contextual Bible Study is a fantastic tool to engage people within a variety of settings from prisons and workplaces to care homes and hospices. It is also a good tool to engage, as the Drewsteignton example showed, non-Christians (though once again a neutral venue, such as the pub, is more likely to encourage participation from this sector than a traditional Bible study in a place of worship). Given the potential variety of settings in which this method can be used, one useful exercise will be to encourage the group to reflect on its collective identity and nature (in all its diversity). A helpful starting point for this is to begin your Contextual Bible Studies with a questionnaire on the place or factors that unite participants. The sharing of responses to these questions could feature as a useful ice-breaking activity prior to the Contextual Bible Studies. Examples of such questions are featured below in a Contextual Bible Study on the Sermon on the Mount. The activity questions have been inspired by Leonora Tubbs Tisdale's community analysis (Tubbs Tisdale 1997:56–90).

Contextual Bible Studies on the Sermon on the Mount

Theme 1: experience and place

Activity: questionnaire

- What in your opinion most distinguishes this place from others?
- What would you define as the boundaries of this place? (These can be social/geographical/vocational or other.)
- Which events/activities most distinguish this place from others?

Read Matthew 5.1–10 and consider the following questions

- Is there anything that immediately jumps off the page at you from this passage?
- What is the significance of a 'mountainside place' in this passage? Does it have an equivalent in your place?
- What do you understand about life experiences captured in this passage? Who are 'the poor in spirit', 'the mourning', 'the meek', 'the hungry', 'the merciful', 'the pure in heart', 'the peace-makers' and 'the persecuted' in your context?
- Collectively write a list of blessings for this place. What images/contexts/people would feature in them?

Theme 2: identity and place

Activity: questionnaire

- Which activities/events in your community/place have been added or emphasized in recent years and what does this tell you about the identity of the place?
- Which activities/events have been abandoned or de-emphasized in recent years and what does this tell you about the identity of the place?

Read Matthew 5.13–14 and consider the following questions

- Is there anything that immediately jumps off the page at you from this passage?

- What characteristics and virtues are implied in the imagery of 'salt' and 'city on a hill' in this passage?
- Who or what can be seen as activities promoting 'salt of the earth', 'salt losing its saltiness', 'light' and 'cities on a hill' in your place?
- If you were to pick images from this place to replace 'salt', 'light' and 'city on a hill' what would they be?

Theme 3: responsibility and place

Activity: questionnaire

- Where in this place is the sacred most identifiable?
- Where in this place do you feel most distant from the sacred?

Read Matthew 6.25–34 and consider the following questions

- Is there anything that immediately jumps off the page at you from this passage?
- What is the function of the images drawn from nature in this passage?
- What 'worries'/threats to sustainability mark this place? In what ways can this passage act as an incentive (and/or disincentive) to responsible action for sustainability of this place?

Theme 4: vision for place

Activity: questionnaire

- Is this place primarily orientated to the past (reliving, longing for glory days) or the future (plans, dreams and visions)?

Read Matthew 7.24–27 and consider the following questions

- Is there anything that immediately jumps off the page at you from this passage?
- What identity or characteristics are drawn in the imagery of the 'house built on the rock' and the 'house built on the sand' in this passage?
- What are the 'houses built on rock' and the 'houses built on sand' in your place?
- What storms and weathers hamper development in this place?
- What in this place would constitute visions built on sand or rock foundations?

Examples of other Contextual Bible Studies

A few other examples of Contextual Bible Studies, drawn from the Gospels of Mark and Luke respectively, based on 'The Parables' and 'Locations' are listed below.

Contextual Bible Studies on the parables

Theme 1: economics of place

Activity

Individually write down on post-it notes effects that the 'credit crunch' and the economic downturn have had in your place. Display all these together on a board and collectively consider both perils and possibilities that these diverse effects pose to the community as a whole.

Read Luke 16.1–9 and consider the following questions

- Is there anything that immediately jumps off the page at you from this passage?
- Who are the equivalents of the 'rich man' and 'manager' in your place?
- What is the significance of the manager's aim to release certain debts so that 'people may welcome me into their homes'?
- What does this parable teach about the economics of generosity and the economics of scarcity? How are these respectively experienced/promoted in your context?

Theme 2: those 'out of place'

Activity

Bring along a variety of local newspapers. Look through the articles to identify individuals/groups who are presented as 'out of place' in some sense. Also consider the criteria by which certain individuals/groups are labelled as such.

Read Luke 14.16–24 and consider the following questions

- Is there anything that immediately jumps off the page at you from this passage?
- What identity or characteristics are respectively shown by the first list of banquet guests (landowner, livestock owner and

bridegroom) and the second list (the poor, crippled, blind and lame)?
- Who or what in this place could be considered 'invited guests' or 'outsiders'?

Theme 3: environment and place

Activity

Imagine that you wake up to find that you have been asleep for two hundred years. In a variety of media (text, poetry, drawing) present what changes to the non-human world and environment you encounter.

Read Luke 12.16–20 and consider the following questions

- Is there anything that immediately jumps off the page at you from this passage?
- What is the attitude of the rich man to the 'earth' in this passage?
- How, if at all, is the 'earth' and 'non-human community' considered in the actions of the human population of this place?

Theme 4: growing the Kingdom in place

Activity

Construct a model of a tree and branches (an old Christmas tree would do). Individually write on cards that can be suspended from the tree's branches characteristics that a true, just and ideal community would exhibit.

Read Luke 13.18–21 and consider the following questions

- Is there anything that immediately jumps off the page at you from this passage?
- What is being communicated about the Kingdom of God through the 'mustard seed' and 'yeast' images?
- What actions in this place could be considered the equivalent of the 'mustard seed' and 'yeast'?

Contextual Bible Studies on locations

Theme 1: houses/homes

Activity

On a piece of paper draw two columns, one marked 'house' and the other 'home'. List various elements/characteristics as you understand it, respective to each category.

Read Mark 2.1–17 and consider the following questions

- Is there anything that immediately jumps off the page at you from this passage?
- What virtues/vices are associated with the house in Capernaum, the tax collector's booth and Levi's house in this story? Can you think of any equivalents of these houses/homes in your place?

Theme 2: temples

Activity

On maps, mark places that act as ideological 'temples' for your community: namely, places where people go to celebrate particular values and worship particular 'gods' that their culture promotes.

Read Mark 11.11–17 and consider the following questions

- Is there anything that immediately jumps off the page at you from this passage?
- What is the role and status of the temple in this passage? What does Jesus imply should be the role of the temple?
- Who or what in this place are its temples? Who or what in this place should be its temples?

Theme 3: kingdoms

Activity

On two identical pictures of boats collectively discuss and draw on the first picture a crew 'divided against themselves' and on the other picture discuss and draw a crew working in harmony.

Read Mark 3.20–27 and consider the following questions

- Is there anything that immediately jumps off the page at you from this passage?

- What do you understand by the concepts of 'a kingdom/house divided against itself'?
- What 'kingdoms divided' risk falling in your context/culture?
- Who are the 'strong men' that threaten your place and how can they be 'bound'?

Theme 4: the tomb

Activity

Divide the group into pairs and ask each pair to share with their partner a particular experience where they have felt trapped by grief, illness etc. As long as all participants are willing, the pairs should then share with the rest of the group the nature of their 'entombing' experiences.

Read Mark 16.1–8 and consider the following questions

- Is there anything that immediately jumps off the page at you from this passage?
- The tomb at the beginning of this story is a place of death, sadness and emptiness. Where are the tomb-like places/experiences in your context?
- What can be done to 'roll the stone away' from those tomb-like places and entombing situations?
- How can 'Easter Triumph' be promoted in a 'Holy Saturday' world?

If you are planning your own Contextual Bible Study it may be worth consulting the following helpful resources in the construction of such activities and questions.

- *The Scottish Bible Society* website has links to 'Conversations', a companion resource for Contextual Bible Study including a text and questions database along with a variety of 'write-up' sessions. Go online to <www.scottishbiblesociety.org> and follow 'Conversations' links.
- *Gerald West and the Ujamaa Centre* have recently produced a resource manual for 'Doing Contextual Bible Study' (2007) which provides texts and questions along with 'write-ups' of sessions: <www.sorat.ukzn.ac.za/ujamaa/ujam123.pdf>.
- *The Urban Theology Unit* website is worth consulting for further links to 'practice'-orientated resources (<www.utusheffield.org.uk>).

Of particular interest is J. Vincent and C. Rowland (eds) *Bible and Practice* (Urban Theology Unit 2001) and J. Vincent, *Outworkings: Gospel Practice and Interpretation* (Urban Theology Unit 2005).

- *Common Ground*, the arts and environmental organization, mentioned in Chapter 3, is a wonderful source of inspiration for activities accompanying Contextual Bible Studies on the theme of 'place'. Their website <www.commonground.org.uk> has plenty of links to discussions regarding parish maps, local distinctiveness, authenticity, sustainability and the importance of food. Why not accompany this survey with a feast of locally produced food, itself contributing to the story of your place?

- *Reflection* is a North American higher education publication that endeavours to provide tools for 'service-learning' of the type I introduced in Chapter 3 of this book. The *Reflection* manual produced by Julie Reed and Christopher Kolbia is available online at <www.uvm.edu/~dewey/reflection_manual>. Chapter 5 is particularly helpful as it offers pointers for a number of group actions that could be adopted within activities accompanying the Contextual Bible Studies. These include information about setting up role plays, quotes, exercises, affinity groups, Frierian fish bowls, guided imagery, life-story activities, and the like.

- The importance of artistic representations for 'embodying' the various responses from group Contextual Bible Studies has been emphasized throughout this project. Poetry writing, photography, map-making, weaving, arts and crafts, dance, music and drama all have important roles not only in allowing people to express themselves in different ways but also, in themselves, becoming place-making and community-making tools. Exegesis 'without words' has an important part to play in the development of place-making sensitivities. Think carefully how different media can be incorporated into your Contextual Bible Study sessions.

The variety of groups and contexts in which this method can be adopted, as this project has attempted to show, is virtually limitless. Many new 'groupings' of churches have found it a useful method to start to build relationships and a common identity. For preachers, Contextual Bible Study is an insightful exercise to do once in a while, not least because it allows an insight into concerns exercising the community at the time. Tubbs Tisdale suggested that a 'folk art' session in which people are encouraged to voice their feelings about a given text could precede a sermon occasionally. In this way the preacher is required 'to do more imaginative work, examining the ordinary world the hearers inhabit, and seeking, like a detective of divinity, to discover the gospel in its midst' (Tubbs Tisdale 1997:131). In the end be as creative, imaginative, experimental and adventurous as you can! Discerning 'the word in place' is a high calling with multiple avenues of possibility.

Bibliography

Abma, T. (2003), 'Learning by Telling: Storytelling Workshops as an Organizational Learning Intervention', *Management Learning* 34, 221–40.

Acheson, J. M. (1981), 'Anthropology of Fishing', *Annual Review of Anthropology* 10, 275–316.

Adamo, T. (2004), 'Psalms' in D. Patte (ed.), *The Global Bible Commentary* (Nashville: Abingdon Press).

Aguilar, M. I. (2002), 'Time Communion and Ancestry in African Biblical Interpretation: A Contextual Note on 1 Maccabees 2:49–70', *Biblical Theology Bulletin* 25, 152–60.

Andrew, T. H. (1921), 'The Cornish Fishing Type', *Man* 21, 137–9.

Ang, T. (2001), 'Foreword' in J. Curno, *Drewsteignton: A Portrait of a Dartmoor Parish and its People* (Tiverton: Halsgrove).

Appardurai, A. (1988), 'Putting Hierarchy in its Place', *Cultural Anthropology* 3, 36–49.

Augé, M. (1995 [1992]), *Non-Places: Introduction to an Anthropology of Supermodernity*, trans. J. Rowe (London: Verso).

Avalos, H. (2007), 'Introducing Sensory Criticism in Biblical Studies: Audiocentricity and Visiocentricity' in Avalos, Melcher and Schipper (eds) (2007), 47–60.

Avalos, H., Melcher, S. and Schipper, J. (eds) (2007), *This Abled Body: Rethinking Disabilities in Biblical Studies* (Atlanta: Society of Biblical Literature).

Bailey, R. (2004), 'Whatever Happened to Good Old White Boys? A Review of the Global Bible Commentary', available online at <www.vanderbilt.edu/AnS/religious_studies/GBC/proscons.htm>.

Bakhtin, M. (1981), *The Dialogic Imagination*, ed. M. Holquist, trans. M. Holquist and C. Emerson (Austin: University of Texas Press).

Basso, K. H. (1996), *Wisdom Sits in Places: Landscapes and Language among the Western Apache* (Albuquerque: University of New Mexico Press).

Batten, A. (2005), 'Studying the Historical Jesus through Service', *Teaching Theology and Religion* 8, 107–13.

Bauckham, R. (2002), *God and the Crisis of Freedom* (Louisville: Westminster John Knox Press).

Bauckham, R. (2003), 'The Eyewitnesses and the Gospel Traditions', *Journal for the Study of the Historical Jesus*, 28–60.

Beldon, C. (2001), 'Giving Voice to Place: Three Models for Understanding American Sacred Space', *Religion and American Culture* 11, 53–81.

155

Bibliography

Bender, B. (1992), 'Theorizing Landscapes, and the Prehistoric Landscapes of Stonehenge', *Man* 27, 735–55.

Bird, S. E. (2002), 'It Makes Sense to Us: Cultural Identity in Local Legends of Place', *Journal of Contemporary Ethnography*, 519–47.

Bishop, M. E. (ed.) (1995), *Religion and Disability: Essays in Scripture, Theology and Ethics* (Kansas: Sheed and Ward).

Blanton, R. (1976), 'Anthropological Studies of Cities', *Annual Review of Anthropology* 5, 249–64.

Blewitt, J. (2005), 'Education for Sustainable Development, Natural Capital and Sustainability: Learning to Last', *Environmental Education Research* 11, 71–82.

Blount, B. (1995), *Cultural Interpretation: Reorienting New Testament Criticism* (Minneapolis: Fortress Press).

Boff, C. (1987), *Theology and Praxis: Epistemological Foundations* (Maryknoll: Orbis Books).

Bookless, D. and Larkin, L. (2006), 'Community and Environment' in Edmondson and Ineson (eds) (2006).

Bornkamm, G. (1963), 'The Stilling of the Storm' in G. Bornkamm, G. Barth and H. J. Held, *Tradition and Interpretation in Matthew* (London: SCM Press), 52–7.

Bouma-Prediger, S. and Walsh, B. (2008), *Beyond Homelessness: Christian Faith in a Culture of Displacement* (Grand Rapids: Eerdmans).

Boyarin, D. (1990), *Intertextuality and the Reading of Midrash* (Indianapolis: Indiana University Press).

Boyarin, J. (1989), 'Voices around the Text: The Ethnography of Reading at Mesivta Tifereth Jerusalem', *Cultural Anthropology* 4, 399–421.

Boyarin, J. (ed.) (1993), *The Ethnography of Reading* (Berkeley and Los Angeles: University of California Press).

Brent Ingram, G. *et al.* (1997), *Queers in Space: Communities, Public Places, Sites of Resistance* (Seattle: Bay Press).

Bridge, G. and Watson, S. (eds) (2000), *A Companion to the City* (Oxford: Blackwell).

Brown, D. (2004), *God and Enchantment of Place* (Oxford: Oxford University Press).

Brueggemann, W. (2002), *The Land: Place as Gift, Promise and Challenge in Biblical Faith* (Minneapolis: Fortress Press).

Brueggemann, W. (2003), *Awed to Heaven, Rooted in Earth* (Minneapolis: Fortress Press).

Bultmann, R. (1960 [1957]), *Existence and Faith: Shorter Writings of Rudolf Bultmann*, trans. S. Ogden (Cleveland: World Meridian).

Butz, D. and Eyles, J. (1997), 'Reconceptualizing Senses of Place: Social Relations, Ideology and Ecology', *Human Geography* 79, 1–25.

Cahill, L. (1990), 'The New Testament and Ethics: Communities of Social Change', *Interpretation* 44, 383–95.

Cameron, H. *et al.* (eds) (2005), *Studying Local Churches: A Handbook* (London: SCM Press).

Cardenal, E. (1978), *The Gospel in Solentiname*, vol. 2, trans. D. Walsh (Maryknoll: Orbis Books).

Cardenal, E. (1982), *The Gospel in Solentiname*, vol. 4, trans. D. Walsh (Maryknoll: Orbis Books).

Carr, D. (2001 [1971]), 'Narrative and the Real World: An Argument for Continuity' in Hinchman and Hinchman (eds) (2001), 7–25.

Carruthers, J. (2007), 'Unpublished Response to L. J. Lawrence, "Being Hefted" ', University of Bristol.

Carter, W. (2000), *Matthew and the Margins* (Maryknoll: Orbis Books).

Casey, E. (1993), *Getting Back into Place* (Bloomington: Indiana University Press).

Cavanaugh, W. (1998), *Torture and Eucharist: Theology, Politics and the Body of Christ* (Oxford: Blackwell).

Church of England (1997), *The Church amongst Deaf People* (London: Church House Publishing).

Cicero (1998), 'An Essay on Old Age' in J. Shelton, *As the Romans Did* (Oxford: Oxford University Press).

Clarke, S. (2002), 'Viewing the Bible through the Eyes and Ears of Subalterns in India', *Biblical Interpretation* 10, 245–66.

Clifford, S. (1996), 'Places, People and Parish Maps' in Clifford and King (eds) (1996), 3–14.

Clifford, S. and King, A. (eds) (1996), *From place to PLACE: maps and Parish Maps* (London: Common Ground).

Clifford, S. and King, A. (2006), *England in Particular: A Celebration of the Commonplace, the Local, the Vernacular and the Distinctive* (London: Hodder and Stoughton).

Cloke, P. *et al.* (2000), 'Homelessness and Rurality: Out of Place in Purified Space?', *Environment and Planning D: Society and Place* 18, 715–35.

Cloke, P., Milbourne, P. and Widdowfield, R. (2002), *Rural Homelessness* (Bristol: Polity Press).

Cocksworth, C. and Brown, R. (2006), *Being a Priest Today* (Norwich: Canterbury Press).

Cone, J. (1997), *God of the Oppressed* (Maryknoll: Orbis Books).

Cooper, N. (2001), 'Tourist or Vagabond', *Political Theology*, vol. 4, 74–90.

Cresswell, T. (1996), *In Place/Out of Place: Geography, Ideology and Transgression* (Minneapolis: University of Minnesota Press).

Cresswell, T. (2004), *Place: A Short Introduction* (Oxford: Blackwell).

Crites, S. (2001 [1971]), 'The Narrative Quality of Experience' in Hinchman and Hinchman (eds) (2001), 26–50.

Croft, S. (ed.) (2006), *The Future of the Parish System: Shaping the Church of England in the 21st Century* (London: Church House Publishing), 3–15.

Crossan, D. and Reed, J. (2001), *Excavating Jesus* (London: SPCK).

Crouch, D. and Matless, D. (1996), 'Reconfiguring Geography: Parish Maps of Common Ground', *Transactions of the Institute of British Geographers* 21, 236–55.

Curno, J. (2001), *Drewsteignton: A Portrait of a Dartmoor Parish and its People* (Tiverton: Halsgrove).

Davie, G. (1994), *Religion in Britain Since 1945: Believing without Belonging* (Oxford: Blackwell).

Davis, L. (1995), *Enforcing Normalcy: Disability, Deafness and the Body* (London: Verso).

Deacon, B. (2004), 'Under Construction: Culture and Regional Formation in South-West England', *European Urban and Regional Studies* 11, 213–25.

Delaney, D. (2005), *Territory: A Short Introduction* (Oxford: Blackwell).

Dietrich, W. and Luz, U. (eds) (2002), *The Bible in a World Context: An Experiment in Contextual Hermeneutics* (Grand Rapids: Eerdmans).

Donaldson, L. E. (2005), 'Gospel Hauntings: The Postcolonial Demons of New Testament Criticism' in Moore and Segovia (eds) (2005), 97–113.

Douglas, M. (1966), *Purity and Danger: An Analysis of Concepts of Pollution and Taboo* (New York: Praeger).

Dube, M. (2000), *Postcolonial Feminist Interpretation of the Bible* (Missouri: Chalice Press).

Edmondson, C. and Ineson, E. (eds) (2006), *Celebrating Community: God's Gift for Today's World* (London: Darton, Longman and Todd).

Edson, M. (2006), 'Community and Conflict' in Edmondson and Ineson (eds) (2006), 111–26.

Eiesland, N. L. (1994), *The Disabled God: Towards a Liberatory Theology of Disability* (Nashville: Abingdon Press).

Ekblad, B. (2005), *Reading the Bible with the Damned* (Louisville: Westminster John Knox Press).

Engberg-Pedersen, T. (ed.) (2001), *Paul Beyond the Judaism/Hellenism Divide* (Louisville: Westminster John Knox Press).

Faith in the City, Report by Archbishop of Canterbury's Commission on Urban Priority Areas (1985) (London: Church House Publishing).

Faithful Cities, Report by the Commission on Urban Life and Faith (2006) (London: Church House Publishing).

Fernandez, J. W. (1974), 'The Mission of Metaphor in Expressive Culture', *Current Anthropology* 15, 119–33.

Fontaine, C. R. (1996), 'Disabilities and Illness in the Bible: A Feminist Perspective' in A. Brenner (ed.), *A Feminist Companion to the Hebrew Bible in the New Testament* (Sheffield: Sheffield Academic Press), 286–300.

Fowl, S. and Jones, G. (1991), *Reading in Communion: Scripture and Ethics in Christian Life* (Grand Rapids: Eerdmans).

Francis, D., Kellaher, L. and Neophytou, G. (2005), *The Secret Cemetery* (Oxford: Berg).

Gibbs, E. and Bolger, R. (2006), *Emerging Churches: Creating Christian Community in Postmodern Cultures* (London: SPCK).

Gnanavaram, M. (1993), 'Dalit Theology and the Parable of the Good Samaritan', *Journal for the Study of the New Testament* 50, 59–83.

Goffman, E. (1963), *Stigma: Notes on the Management of Spoiled Identity* (New York: Simon and Schuster).

Gorringe, T. (2002), *A Theology of the Built Environment: Justice, Empowerment, Redemption* (Cambridge: Cambridge University Press).

Gorringe, T. (2006), *Harvest: Food, Farming and the Churches* (London: SPCK).

Gorringe, T. (2007), 'Blackbird Leys: A Non-Place Urban Realm' (unpublished paper).

Graham, E., Walton, H. and Ward, F. (2005), *Theological Reflection: Methods* (London: SCM Press).

Gripaios, P., Gripaios, R. and Munday, M. (1997), 'The Role of Inward Investment in Urban Economic Development: The Cases of Bristol, Cardiff and Plymouth', *Urban Studies* 34, 579–603.

Habel, N. C. (ed.) (2000), *Readings from the Perspective of the Earth: Earth Bible Volume 1* (Sheffield: Sheffield Academic Press).

Hale, A. (2001), 'Representing the Cornish: Contesting Heritage Interpretation in Cornwall', *Tourist Studies* 1, 185–96.

Handelman, H. (1982), *The Slayers of Moses: The Emergence of Rabbinic Interpretation in Modern Literary Theory* (Albany: State University of New York Press).

Hanson, K. C. and Oakman, D. (1998), *Palestine in the Time of Jesus: Social Structures and Social Conflicts* (Minneapolis: Fortress Press).

Hauerwas, S. (2004), 'Community and Diversity: The Tyranny of Normality' in J. Swinton (ed.), *Theology of Disability: Disabling Society, Enabling Theology* (Birmingham NY: The Haworth Pastoral Press), 37–43.

Healey, P. (2002), 'On Creating the City as a Collective Resource', *Urban Studies* 39, 1777–92.

Hinchman, L. P. and Hinchman, S. K. (eds) (2001), *Memory, Identity and Community: The Idea of Narrative in the Human Sciences* (New York: State University of New York Press).

Hind Report: Formation of Ministry within a Learning Church (2003) available online at <www.cofe.anglican.org/lifeevents/ministry/workofmindiv/tetc/safwp/hindreport2003.html>.

Hitching, P. (2003), *The Church and Deaf People* (Milton Keynes: Paternoster Press).

Houlden, L. (1990), 'Editorial', *Theology* 93 (London: SPCK).

Howard-Brook, W. and Gwyther, A. (2001), *Unveiling Empire: Reading Revelation Then and Now* (Maryknoll: Orbis Books).

Hull, J. (2001), *In the Beginning there was Darkness: A Blind Person's Conversations with the Bible* (London: SCM Press).

Humphrey, C. (1999), 'Shamans in the City', *Anthropology Today* 15, 3–10.

Hunt, G. and Satterlee, S. (1986), 'Cohesion and Division: Drinking in an English Village', *Man* 21, 521–37.

Hutchinson, N. (2006), 'Disabling Beliefs? Impaired Embodiment in the Religious Tradition of the West', *Body and Society*, vol. 12, no. 4, 1–23.

Inge, J. (2003), *A Christian Theology of Place* (Aldershot: Ashgate).

Irizarry, J. (2003), 'The Religious Educator as Cultural Spec-actor: Researching Self in Intercultural Pedagogy', *Religious Education* 98, 365–81.

Jedrej, M. C. (1996), 'Time and Space' in A. Barnard and J. Spencer (eds) (1996), *Encyclopedia of Social and Cultural Anthropology* (London: Routledge), 547–50.

Jennings, S. (2007), 'Ordinary Reading in Extraordinary Times: A Jamaican Love Story' in West (ed.) (2007b), 49–62.

Keener, C. (1999), *A Commentary on the Gospel of Matthew* (Grand Rapids: Eerdmans).

Kerr, T. (2006), 'Land as Subaltern', *Limina*, vol. 12, 40–51.

Kong, L. (2001), 'Religion and Technology: Refiguring Place, Space, Identity and Community', *Area* 33, 404–13.

Kong, L. (2004), 'Religion and Technology: Refiguring Place, Space, Identity and Community', *Area* 33, 404–13.

Koyama, K. (1993), 'Christ's Homelessness', *The Christian Century*, 702–3.

Kunstler, J. (1993), *The Geography of Nowhere: The Rise and Decline of America's Man-Made Landscape* (New York: Simon and Schuster).

Kyle, G. and Woll, B. (1988), *Sign Language: The Study of Deaf People and their Language* (Cambridge: Cambridge University Press).

Ladd, P. (2003), *Understanding Deaf Culture: In Search of Deafhood* (Clevedon: Multilingual Matters).

Lane, B. (1998), *The Solace of Fierce Landscapes* (Oxford: Oxford University Press).

Langrish, M. (2004), 'Dynamics of Community' in J. Martineau *et al.*, *Changing Rural Life* (Norwich: Canterbury Press), 21–43.

Latvus, K. (2007), 'The Bible in British Urban Theology: An Analysis by a Finnish Companion' in West (ed.) (2007b), 133–40.

Laviolett, P. (2003), 'Landscaping Death: Resting Places for Cornish Identity', *Journal of Material Culture* 8, 215–40.

Lawrence, L. J. (2006), 'Scribes Trained for the Kingdom of Heaven: Reflections on Reading the Bible for Politics in Community, Secondary and Higher Education Contexts in Scotland', *Discourse* 5, 99–122.

Lawrence, L. J. (2007a), 'Being Hefted: Reflections on Place, Stories and Contextual Bible Study', *Expository Times* 118, 530–5.

Lawrence, L. J. (2007b), 'On a Cliff's Edge: Actualizing Luke 8.22–39 in an Intentional Christian Community on the North Devon Coast', *Expository Times* 119, 111–15.

Lawrence, L. J. (2008), 'Contextual Bible Studies: Resources on Place', *Expository Times* 120, 131–2.

Lawrence, L. J. (2009), 'The Stilling of the Sea and the Imagination of Place in a Cornish Fishing Village', *Expository Times* 121, 172–7.

Lee, K. S. (2004), 'Lamentations' in Patte (ed.) (2004).

Lees, J. (2007), *Word of Mouth: Using the Remembered Bible for Building Community* (Glasgow: Wild Goose Publications).

Lefebvre, H. (1991), *The Production of Space* (Oxford: Blackwell).

Lewis, H. (2007), *Deaf Liberation Theology* (Aldershot: Ashgate).

Lieu, J. (1997), *The Gospel of Luke* (London: Epworth).

Liew, T. (2004), 'Acts' in Patte (ed.) (2004).

Liew, T. (2006), 'Tyranny, Boundary and Might: Colonial Mimicry in Mark's Gospel' in Sugirtharajah (ed.) (2006), 206–23.

Linde, C. (2000), 'The Acquisition of a Speaker by a Story: How History Becomes Memory and Identity', *Ethos* 28, 608–32.

Linde, C. (2001), 'Narrative and Social Tacit Knowledge', *Journal of Knowledge Management* 5, 160–70.

Low, S. M. and Lawrence, D. (1990), 'The Built Environment and Spatial Form', *American Review of Anthropology* 19, 453–505.

Low, S. M. and Lawrence-Zuniga, D. (eds) (2003), *The Anthropology of Space and Place: Locating Culture* (Oxford: Blackwell).

Low, S. (1996), 'The Anthropology of Cities: Imaging and Theorizing the City', *Annual Review of Anthropology* 25, 385–409.

Lumbala, F. K. (1998), *Celebrating Jesus Christ in Africa: Liturgy and Inculturation* (Maryknoll: Orbis Books).

Macintyre, B. (2007), 'Are You Hefted? If Not that's a Pity', *Times*, available online at <www.timesonline.co.uk/tol/comment/colunists/ben_Macintyre/article1289605.ece>.

Mackey, S. (2002), 'Drama, Landscape and Memory', *Research in Drama Education* 7, 9–25.

Macy, J. (1993), *Thinking Like a Mountain: Towards a Council of All Beings* (Philadelphia: New Society Publishers).

Malbon, E. S. (1986), *Narrative Space and Mythic Meaning in Mark* (Sheffield: Sheffield Academic Press).

Mannur, A. (2003), 'Postscript: Cyberspaces and the Interfacing of Diasporas' in J. E. Braziel and A. Mannur (eds) (2003), *Theorizing Diaspora* (Oxford: Blackwell), 283–90.

Markusen, A. (2004), 'The Work of Forgetting and Remembering Places', *Urban Studies* 41/12, 2303–13.

Martineau, J. F., Francis, L. J. and Francis, P. (2004), *Changing Rural Life: A Christian Response to Key Rural Issues* (Norwich: Canterbury Press).

Mbiti, J. (1975 [1969]), *African Religions and Philosophy* (Austin: Holt, Rinehart and Winston).

McDonough, P. (1998), 'Presenting the Word of God in Sign Language' in P. McDonough (ed.), *Ephphata: Proceedings from the International Catholic Deaf Religious Conference* (Monmouth: A & K Publications), 55–80.

McFague, S. (1974), 'Parable, Metaphor and Theology', *Journal of the American Academy of Religion* 42, 630–45.

McHugh, K. (2003), 'Three Faces of Ageism: Society, Image and Place', *Ageing and Society* 23, 165–85.

McKim, D. K. (ed.) (1998), *Historical Handbook of Major Biblical Interpreters* (Illinois: InterVarsity Press).

Meeks, W. (1993), *The Origins of Christian Morality: The First Two Centuries* (New Haven and London: Yale University Press).

Melcher, S. J. (2007), 'With Whom Do the Disabled Associate? Metaphorical Interplay in the Latter Prophets' in Avalos, Melcher and Schipper (eds) (2007), 115–30.

Melia, S. (2002), *Hallsands: A Village Betrayed* (Newton Abbot: Forest Publishing).

Mercer, J. A. (2005), 'Teaching the Bible in Congregations: A Congregational Studies Pedagogy for Contextual Education', *Religious Education Association* 100, 2802–95.

Moore, S. (1995), 'True Confessions and Weird Obsessions: Autobiographical Interventions in Literary and Biblical Studies', *Semeia* 72, 19–51.

Moore, S. (2006), 'Mark and Empire: Zealot and Postcolonial Readings' in Sugirtharajah (ed.) (2006), 193–205.

Moore, S. and Segovia, F. (eds) (2005), *Postcolonial Biblical Criticism: Interdisciplinary Intersections* (London: T&T Clark).

Morphy, H. and Morphy, F. (2006), 'Tasting the Waters: Discriminating Identities in the Water of Blue Mud Bay', *Journal of Material Culture* 11, 67–85.

Mosala, I. (1989), *Biblical Hermeneutics and Black Theology in South Africa* (Grand Rapids: Eerdmans).

Moxnes, H. (2003), *Putting Jesus in his Place: A Radical Vision of Household and Kingdom* (Louisville: Westminster John Knox Press).

Musopole, A. C. (1993), 'Witchcraft Terminology, the Bible and African Christian Theology: An Exercise in Hermeneutics', *Journal of Religion in Africa* 23, 347–54.

Myers, C. (2006), 'Mark 13 in a Different Imperial Context' in Vincent (ed.) (2006).

Myers, C. *et al.* (1996), *Say to This Mountain: Mark's Story of Discipleship* (Maryknoll: Orbis Books).

Nelavala, S. (2006), 'Smart Syrophoenician Woman: A Dalit Feminist Reading of Mark 7.24–31', *Expository Times* 118, 64–9.

Newby, H. (1977), *The Deferential Worker* (London: Allen Lane).

Nixon, D. and Mawhinney, L. (2005), 'The Faith and Quality of Life Strategy: Strengthening Our Community's Faith and Quality of Life'.

Northcott, M. (2008), 'Eucharistic Eating and Why Many Early Christians Preferred Fish' in D. Grumett and R. Muers (eds) (2008), *Eating and Believing: Interdisciplinary Perspectives on Vegetarianism and Theology* (London: T&T Clark), 232–46.

Novak, M. (1975), 'Story and Experience' in J. B. Wiggins (ed.) (1975), *Religion as Story* (Lanham: University of America Press), 175–97.

Origen (1990), *Homilies on Leviticus 1–16*, trans. G. W. Barkley, *Fathers of the Church* 83 (Washington: Catholic University of America Press).

Patte, D. (ed.) (2004), *The Global Bible Commentary* (Nashville: Abingdon Press).

Paulsen, K. (2004), 'Making Character Concrete: Empirical Strategies for Studying Place Distinction', *City and Community* 3, 243–62.

Peden, A. (2005), 'Contextual Bible Study at Cornton Vale Women's Prison, Stirling', *Expository Times* 117, 15–18.

Percy, M. (2006), 'Many Rooms in my Father's House: The Changing Identity of the English Parish Church' in Croft (ed.) (2006), 3–15.

Peterson, E. H. (2002), *The Message: The Bible in Contemporary Language* (Colorado Springs: Navpress).

Pohl, C. (1999), *Making Room: Recovering Hospitality as a Christian Tradition* (Grand Rapids: Eerdmans).

Pritchard, J. (2007), *The Life and Work of a Priest* (London: SPCK).

Raja, M. (2000), 'Reading Bible from a Dalit Location: Some Points for Interpretation', *Voices From the Third World* 33, 71–91.

Ramachandra, V. (2008), *Subverting Global Myths: Theology and Public Issues Shaping our World* (London: SPCK).

Reed, A. (2002), 'City of Details: Interpreting the Personality of London', *The Journal of the Royal Anthropological Institute* 8, 127–41.

Relph, E. (1976), *Place and Placelessness* (London: Pion).

Reynolds, T. E. (2008), *Vulnerable Communion: A Theology of Disability and Hospitality* (Grand Rapids: Brazos Press).

Richard, P. (2004), 'Jesus: A Latin American Perspective' in Patte (ed.) (2004).

Riches, J. (2005), 'Worship Resources, Contextual Bible Study: Some Reflections', *The Expository Times* 117, 23–6.

Riches, J. and Miller, S. (2006), 'Popular Readings of Mark' in Vincent (ed.) (2006), 109–25.

Ricoeur, P. (1995), *Figuring the Sacred: Religion, Narrative and Imagination* (Minneapolis: Fortress Press).

Riley, M. and Harvey, D. (2005), 'Landscape Archaeology, Heritage and the Community in Devon: An Oral History Approach', *International Journal of Heritage Studies* 11, 269–88.

Riley, M. and Harvey, D. (2007), 'Talking Geography: On Oral History and the Practice of Geography', *Social and Cultural Geography* 8, 345–52.

Rodman, M. (1992), 'Empowering Place: Multilocality and Multivocality', *American Anthropologist* 94, 640–56.

Rodway-Dyer, S. and Shaw, G. (2005), 'The Effects of the Foot-and-Mouth Outbreak on Visitor Behaviour: The Case of Dartmoor National Park, South-West England', *Journal of Sustainable Tourism* 13.1, 63–81.

Rose, G. (1993), *Feminism and Geography: The Limits of Geographical Knowledge* (Cambridge: Polity Press).

Rotenberg, M. (1986), 'The Midrash and Biographic Rehabilitation', *Journal for the Scientific Study of Religion* 25, 41–55.

Rowland, C. (2000), 'The Engraver, The Chandler and the Trade Unionist: Reflections on the Grassroots Reading of Scripture', *Political Theology* 2, 11–32.

Rowland, C. (2006a), 'What Have We Got Here?' in Vincent (ed.) (2006), 3–8.

Rowland, C. (2006b), 'Practical Exegesis' in Vincent (ed.) (2006), 22–5.

Ryken, L., Wilhoit, J. C. and Longman, T. (eds) (1998), *Dictionary of Biblical Imagery* (Illinois: InterVarsity Press).

Saxbee, J. (2004), 'A Country Retreat' in J. Martineau *et al.* (2004), *Changing Rural Life: A Christian Response to Key Rural Issues* (Norwich: Canterbury Press), 6–20.

Schama, S. (1995), *Landscape and Memory* (London: Fontana Press).

Schipper, J. (2007), 'Disabling Israelite Leadership: 2 Samuel 6:23 and Other Images of Disability in the Deuteronomistic History' in Avalos, Melcher and Schipper (eds) (2007), 103–14.

Schneider, J. and Susser, I. (2003), *Wounded Cities: Destruction and Reconstruction in a Globalized World* (Oxford: Berg).

Sedgwick, P. (ed.) (1995), *God in the City: Essays and Reflections from the Archbishop's Urban Theology Group* (London: Mowbray).

Segovia, F. (1995), 'Cultural Studies and Contemporary Biblical Criticism: Ideological Criticism as Mode of Discourse' in Segovia and Tolbert (eds) (1995b), 1–17.

Segovia, F. and Tolbert, M. A. (eds) (1995a), *Reading from this Place*, vol. 1 (Minneapolis: Fortress Press).

Segovia, F. and Tolbert, M. A. (eds) (1995b), *Reading from this Place*, vol. 2 (Minneapolis: Fortress Press).

Senghas, J. and Monaghan, L. (2002), 'Signs of their Times: Deaf Communities and the Culture of Language', *Annual Review of Anthropology* 31, 69–97.

Sheldrake, P. (2001), *Spaces for the Sacred: Place, Memory and Identity* (Baltimore: Johns Hopkins University Press).

Shelton, J. (1998), *As the Romans Did* (Oxford: Oxford University Press).

Sherwood, Y. (2000), *A Biblical Text and its Afterlives: The Survival of Jonah in Western Culture* (Cambridge: Cambridge University Press).

Sibley, D. (1995), *Geographies of Exclusion: Society and Difference in the West* (London: Routledge).

Sil, G. (1996), *A Handbook of Symbols in Christian Art* (New York: Touchstone).

Smith, J. Z. (1987), *To Take Place: Toward Theory in Ritual* (Chicago: University of Chicago Press).

Speth, J. (2004), *Red Sky at Morning: America and the Crisis of the Global Environment* (New Haven: Yale University Press).

Stanton, W. (2005), 'Interview', *Exeter News* 10.

Stegemann, E. and Stegemann, W. (1999), *The Jesus Movement: A Social History of its First Century* (Edinburgh: T&T Clark).

Stern, D. (1988), 'Midrash and Indeterminacy', *Critical Enquiry* 15, 132–61.

Stewart, E. (2005), *Gathered Around Jesus: An Alternative Spatial Practice in Mark*, PhD dissertation, University of Notre Dame.

Stewart, E. (2007), 'The City in Mark: Reflections on a Spatial Theme' in A. Hagedorn, Z. Crook and E. Stewart (eds) (2007), *In Other Words: Essays on Social Science Methods and the New Testament in Honor of Jerome H. Neyrey* (Sheffield: Sheffield Phoenix), 202–20.

Strang, V. (2004), *The Meaning of Water* (Oxford: Berg).

Sugirtharajah, R. (2003), 'Loitering with Intent: Biblical Text in Public Places', *Biblical Interpretation* 11, 566–78.

Sugirtharajah, R. (ed.) (2006), *The Postcolonial Biblical Reader* (Oxford: Blackwell).

Tannehill, R. C. (1996), *Luke* (Nashville: Abingdon Press).

Thompson, P. (2000), *The Voice of the Past: Oral History* (Oxford: Oxford University Press).

Tilley, C. Y. (2006), 'Landscape, Heritage and Identity', *Journal of Material Culture* 11, 7–32.

Tuan, Y. (1974), *Topophilia: A Study of Environmental Perception, Attitudes and Values* (Englewood Cliffs: Prentice-Hall).

Tuan, Y. (1977), *Space and Place: The Perspective of Experience* (Minneapolis: University of Minnesota Press).

Tubbs Tisdale, L. (1997), *Preaching as Local Theology and Folk Art* (Minneapolis: Fortress Press).

Tyler, S. A. (1986), 'On Being Out of Words', *Cultural Anthropology* 2, 131–7.

van Ginkel, R. (2008), *Coastal Cultures: An Anthropology of Fishing and Whaling* (Apeldoorn: Het Spinhuis).

Vanhoozer, K. (2002), *First Theology: God, Scripture and Hermeneutics* (Downers Grove: InterVarsity Press).

Vincent, J. (ed.) (2006), *Mark: Gospel of Action, Personal and Community Responses* (London: SPCK).

Ward, G. (2000), *Cities of God* (London: Routledge).

West, G. (1996), 'Reading the Bible Differently: Giving Shape to the Discourses of the Dominated', *Semeia* 73, 21–41.

West, G. (1999), *The Academy of the Poor: Toward a Dialogical Reading of the Bible* (Sheffield: Sheffield Academic Press).

West, G. (2003), 'The Bible in the Light of HIV/AIDS in South Africa', *Ecumenical Review*, 335–44.

West, G. (2004), 'Beyond the Critical Curtain: Community-Based Service Learning in an African Context', *Teaching Theology and Religion* 7, 71–82.

West, G. (ed.) (2007a), '(Ac)Claiming the (Extra)ordinary Reader of the Bible' in West (ed.) (2007a), *Reading Other-Wise: Socially Engaged Biblical Scholars Reading with Their Local Communities* (Atlanta: SBL), 29–48.

West, G. (ed.) (2007b), *Reading Other-Wise: Socially Engaged Biblical Scholars Reading with their Local Communities* (Atlanta: SBL).

West, G. and Ujamaa Centre Staff (2007), 'Doing Contextual Bible Study Resource Manual', available online at <www.sorat.ukzn.ac.za/ujamaa/ujam123.pdf>.

Wilson, S. M. and Peterson, L. C. (2002), 'The Anthropology of Online Communities', *Annual Review of Anthropology* 31, 449–67.

Williams, M. (2003), 'Why is Cornwall Poor? Poverty and Migration since the 1960s', *Journal of Contemporary History*, vol. 17, no. 3, 55–70.

Williams, R. (2000), *On Christian Theology* (Oxford: Blackwell).

Winter, S. (2001), 'Tackling Social Exclusion', *Political Theology* 4, 65–73.

Worster, A. and Abrams, E. (2005), 'Sense of Place among New England Commercial Fishermen and Organic Farmers: Implications for Socially Constructed Environmental Education', *Environmental Education Research* 11, 525–35.

Yarchin, W. (2004), *History of Biblical Interpretation: A Reader* (Peabody: Hendrickson).

Index

167